Sewing Patterns
200 Q&A

Sewing Patterns

200 Q&A

Questions answered on everything from understanding patterns to making alterations

Sophie English

To Mim, for your patience, love, and guiding hands.

All inquiries should be addressed to:
Barron's Educational Series, Inc.
250 Wireless Boulevard
Hauppauge, New York 11788
www.barronseduc.com

ISBN: 978-0-7641-6453-8

Library of Congress Control Number: 2011931596

This book is published and produced by
Quantum Books
6 Blundell Street
London N7 9BH

QUMSP26

Publisher: Sarah Bloxham
Managing Editor: Julie Brooke
Editor: Caroline Smith
Project Editor: Samantha Warrington
Assistant Editor: Jo Morley
Design: Dave Jones
Photographer: Marcos Bevilacqua
Production: Rohana Yusof

Printed in China by Midas Printing International Ltd.

9 8 7 6 5 4 3 2 1

CONTENTS

Introduction   6

Chapter 1:   Essential Equipment and Choosing Fabric   8
Chapter 2:   Choosing and Understanding Patterns   34
Chapter 3:   Taking Measurements and Getting a Good Fit   56
Chapter 4:   Preparing the Pattern and Fabric   78
Chapter 5:   Adjusting Bodices and Tops   102
Chapter 6:   Adjusting Waistlines and Skirts   124
Chapter 7:   Adjusting Sleeves and Armholes   144
Chapter 8:   Adjusting Pants   162
Chapter 9:   Further Ways to Create and Adapt Patterns   190
Chapter 10:   Achieving a Professional-Looking Finish   204

Glossary   220
Index   222
Acknowledgments   224

INTRODUCTION

I think I made my first skirt when I was about thirteen or fourteen years old. The fit and the workmanship was a little shaky and I enjoyed the process, but I never wore the skirt! At that time, in the 1980s, sewing skills were still being taught at school and I liked the classes, in fact needlework was probably the only subject I was good at. With a combination of school lessons and some help from my grandmother, I started—but didn't always finish—various sewing projects, learning a little about commercial patterns and how to put together a garment along the way.

My first sewing success was making a dress to go to a dance when I was about eighteen years old. I produced a very simple, bias-cut, silk-satin slip-dress in jade green, which I loved, fitted well, and was admired by many. The feeling was fantastic and from that moment I knew I wanted to be involved in fashion and clothing.

I have always been more interested in the art of clothing construction and fit, rather than following fashion itself and the latest catwalk trends. I realized I had to get some technical skills in order to achieve the designs I wanted. I chose to go to the London College of Fashion since courses there concentrated on giving students practical skills in pattern making, garment construction, and tailoring.

I left college and started to work for designers such as Nicole Farhi and Edina Ronay, where I gained valuable experience. However, I quickly realized I wanted to design my own collection. I started to design evening wear and sold pieces to a shop on Fulham Road in London, the owner of which also ran the wedding-dress department at Harrods.

My love of 1930s style, bias-cut, fluid evening dresses, as well as luxurious silk and satin fabrics, easily translated into designing wedding dresses and I started my business— www.sophieenglish.co.uk—selling to shops such as Harrods and Liberty, in London, as well as Kleinfeld, in New York. After ten years running a bridal-wear business and juggling life with two small daughters, I decided to have a break. Having recharged my batteries, a chance meeting with a restaurant manager has led my design skills toward a new direction—designing staff uniforms for restaurants, hotels, and health spas, with clients like The Dorchester and Harvey Nichols, who want well-designed and practical outfits for their staff.

After twenty years of working in this industry, the one area that still fascinates me is the fit of clothing. How each person and his or her body shape differs, even though he or she can have standard-size measurements. Wearing a well-fitting garment is incredibly flattering and possibly more important than whether the style is fashionable.

You have probably already noticed that buying clothes can be a hit-and-miss affair, especially if you are tall, petite, or simply don't like the current fashion. The beauty of making your own clothes means you have the chance to own, say, a dress that fits properly or a shirt with sleeves the right length. By making clothes with commercial sewing patterns you can adapt these to fit any figure type and successfully make your own clothes.

Whether you are a novice or experienced at making clothes, I hope

Chapters 5 to 8 of this book show you how to adapt commercial sewing patterns. For clarity and ease, we have photocopied the patterns we used. You can, of course, make your alterations to tissue-paper patterns. That said, photocopying a pattern can be a good idea; if you make a mistake you won't have cut up the original pattern!

Where extra paper has been inserted in a pattern, we have used red paper since it will show up, and we have used red pen to draw in lines. You can use ordinary paper and pencils for the same tasks.

If any examples of sewing have been shown, the stitching has been done in a contrasting color thread so that it shows in the photographs. In reality, we would suggest you always use a matching color thread for your final stitching.

this book solves some of your pattern problems as well as giving you a few industry tips and shortcuts.

1. Which basic tools do I need to start?

2. Which types of scissors do I need?

3. Are there any other cutting tools I need?

4. How essential is it to have a tailor's dummy or dress form?

5. Which are the best measuring tools to use?

6. What sort of paper do I need to adapt a commercial pattern?

7. Do I need a curved ruler?

8. What should I use to transfer pattern information to the pieces of fabric?

9. Which are the best markers for fabric?

10. Do I need an expensive sewing machine?

11. Do I need an overlocker?

12. Which sewing machine accessories will I need?

13. How important is pressing?

14. Will an ordinary iron and ironing board do?

15. How do I choose the right fabric?

16. Do I choose natural or synthetic fabric?

17. Do I choose woven or knit fabrics?

18. When should I choose jersey or other stretch fabrics?

19. Is it easy to use checked, plaid, or patterned fabrics?

20. I've been given some silk; what could I make out of it?

21. What should I use for lining?

22. What sort of interlining should I use?

23. Which threads should I choose?

24. What sort of buttons and other fasteners should I choose?

25. What sort of zipper should I use?

1

ESSENTIAL EQUIPMENT AND CHOOSING FABRIC

Question 1:
Which basic tools do I need to start?

If you are planning to start making your own clothes and, therefore, start using sewing patterns, there are a few basic tools that will be essential. To start with, you need scissors—for cutting paper and fabric. You'll find more information on the best cutting tools to use in Questions 2 and 3.

If you are planning on making clothes on a regular basis, then a sewing machine will be essential. To find out more about sewing machines and their accessories, look at Questions 10 to 12.

Pins are vital for pinning the pattern to your fabric. And, of course, they are needed for holding together the parts of your garment as you sew. Buy good-quality sharp pins; they work just as well on pattern paper as they do on fabrics,

so you can use the same type for all your dressmaking jobs.

You will also need a range of different-sized needles for any hand sewing. You need to match the needle to the job—so if you're working with a fine fabric, use a fine needle. And if you're trying to sew through a thick chunky fabric, then

ABOVE Pins come with a range of different heads. Ball-headed pins, with their colored glass heads, are useful since they are easy to see.

EXPERT TIP

66 An old-fashioned pincushion is still a perfect place to keep pins; they're easily picked out of the cushion and the tips are protected by being pushed into the padding. The type that is held on the wrist can be very useful—the pins are always on hand and you don't have to fumble for a pin at a crucial moment during the pattern-cutting or sewing process. Keep a magnet handy for picking up any that you drop. 99

you'll need a thick, sturdy needle to do the job properly. Ideally, a needle should be sharp enough to easily pierce the fabric but it shouldn't be so thick that it damages the material and leaves holes.

And last, but not least, you will need a tape measure. The key to using sewing patterns successfully is to take accurate measurements, and you can do this only with a good-quality, well-marked tape measure.

Question 2:
Which types of scissors do I need?

You will need scissors for cutting fabric and scissors for cutting paper patterns. It's important to never use your fabric scissors to cut paper, and vice versa, since both types will become blunt very quickly if you do.

As long as you have a pair of scissors sharp enough to cut fabric then any style will do. However, dressmaking shears are ideal since the handle and blade are angled in such a way as to make it easier to cut out fabric that's been laid out flat. Heavy shears, 8–10 inches (21–26 cm) long are a good choice since they allow smooth progress through most fabrics. In a professional couture pattern-cutting workroom they will keep several pairs of scissors, reserving a pair for each type of fabric since different materials blunt the blades at different rates; silk, for example, tends to blunt scissors more rapidly than wool.

An ordinary pair of scissors will be fine for cutting out patterns. But, as with fabric scissors, it is vital not to use them for anything else other than paper or card stock.

ABOVE A pair of ordinary scissors that you set aside just for pattern cutting will be an invaluable part of your dressmaking kit.

Question 3:
Are there any other cutting tools I need?

If you have a pair of dressmaking scissors, then you really don't need any other kind of cutting tool for cutting out fabric. However, if you have completed craft projects such as quilting you may be familiar with rotary cutters. This "pizza cutter" for fabric is a fast, sharp tool, which is useful for cutting straight lines. The advantage is that the cutter can be used to cut up to eight layers of fabric. However, it doesn't have the flexibility for use on curved areas such as armholes. A rotary cutter needs to be used in conjunction with a self-healing mat or it will damage the surface onto which you are cutting.

While dressmaking shears are perfect for fabric, they are large and heavy and can be awkward to use for cutting out and snipping into small areas. A pair of sharp, small, embroidery scissors are ideal.

Pinking shears are also very handy. The special serrated blade cuts a zigzag edge along fabric that won't fray as quickly as a straight cut edge.

And for those times when you make a mistake, and need to undo any stitching, then a seam ripper is an invaluable tool.

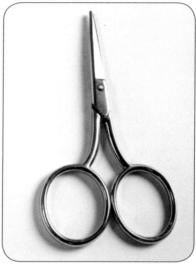

ABOVE Embroidery scissors are useful when you are cutting into small, detailed areas of a sewing pattern, such as armholes and necklines.

Question 4:
How essential is it to have a tailor's dummy or dress form?

If you're making a garment that has a reasonably loose fit and you can fit it on yourself or on a similar-sized friend, then a tailor's dummy isn't essential.

However, if you have a more ambitious project such as fitting a dress, then it becomes increasingly difficult to get the fit right on yourself; you won't be able to see the back view properly or be able to adjust the hem accurately. This is when a dummy or dress form is vital. A dummy can also be very useful when making a garment to see how a sleeve is hanging or whether a collar is sitting correctly.

There are two types of dummy: an adjustable dress form that can be easily altered to your measurements and bought relatively inexpensively, and a fixed-measurement dummy, manufactured for the fashion industry and sold in a variety of standard sizes. Occasionally you might find a cheap fixed-measurement dummy which may not be to your measurements but if smaller could be padded out to your shape.

ABOVE A modern tailor's dummy can be adjusted at key points to mirror your shape and proportions.

Question 5:
Which are the best measuring tools to use?

A flexible, good-quality, plastic tape measure that doesn't stretch is an invaluable tool in any dressmaking kit. You will need your tape measure to take measurements of your body and to measure pattern pieces and parts of the garment before they are sewn in. Taking accurate measurements is an essential part of getting a good fit. A tape measure should measure at least 60 inches (150 cm) long with both imperial and metric measurements marked. A wooden or metal yardstick is also very useful; you can use it to ensure hems are level. When you try a skirt on a tailor's dummy, you can use the yardstick to measure up from the ground at intervals to make sure the hem is even all around. It's also handy when you're working with sewing patterns laid out on a flat surface such as a table or floor, since a tape measure (which is usually stored rolled up) won't lie as flat.

ABOVE A tape measure is an essential yet inexpensive part of any sewing kit. Keep it neatly rolled up to help reduce wear and tear.

Question 6:
What sort of paper do I need to adapt a commercial pattern?

When altering a commercial pattern it is sometimes necessary to attach another bit of paper to a pattern piece in order to extend a hem, say, or widen the hip area. Cheap printer paper is usually fine for this, but tracing paper can be useful if you need to mirror adjustments from one pattern piece to another.

If you would like to significantly modify a pattern, then it might be better to use special pattern paper, which is sold plain or marked with a grid, or with dots and crosses. The marked papers are useful for lining up grain lines as well as making it easier to draw in style lines and square up pattern pieces.

When attaching commercial pattern pieces use masking tape. Cellophane tape is unforgiving and seems to bunch together the fine tissue paper that commercial patterns are made of, and it is virtually impossible to remove without ripping the paper.

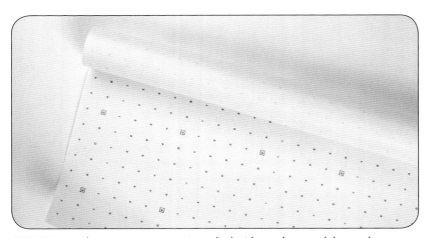

ABOVE Dot and cross-pattern paper is marked with evenly spaced dots and crosses, making it easier to transfer information from commercial sewing patterns accurately.

Question 7:
Do I need a curved ruler?

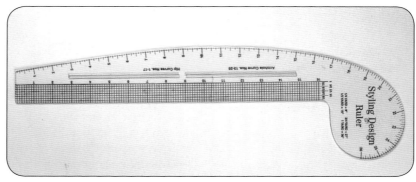

ABOVE A curved ruler is designed so that the edge becomes gradually tighter and more rounded in the curve.

For really simple pattern alterations you can use a standard, straight ruler but if you want to make more complex adjustments to sewing patterns, then a curved ruler is a very useful addition to your measuring equipment. Such rulers are also known as styling design rulers or patternmasters.

The curved edges of the ruler are invaluable if you need to draw in new lines when altering patterns at the hip, bust, and armhole— anywhere, in fact, where there is a curved line. The ruler also features a straight edge, so you can use it as a conventional ruler. It is also marked with measuring lines to help you adjust and add seam allowances. This is useful if you have purchased a brand of pattern which doesn't include seam allowances.

Question 8:
What should I use to transfer pattern information to the pieces of fabric?

The main aim when cutting out a sewing pattern is to transfer information from the pattern onto the fabric; information that is essential when it comes to sewing together the garment.

On the pattern you will see markings that denote features (such as darts) and the position of other adjoining garment pieces (such as collars, pockets, and facings). Traditionally, these markings are transferred to the fabric with tailor's tacks—temporary loose basting stitches sewn through the layers of fabric and cut apart when the pattern is removed. A simpler method is to mark the desired points with a suitable marker on the wrong side of the fabric.

Pin the pattern pieces to the fabric and carefully cut around each one, keeping the pattern as flat and as still as possible to make sure there is no fabric distortion. Transfer the pattern markings to the fabric once the pieces have been cut out.

Question 9:
Which are the best markers for fabric?

Traditionally, tailor's chalk is used to transfer the pattern information to the fabric since the chalk marks can be brushed easily away once the fabric parts are assembled. It comes in a variety of forms and in various colors. You buy triangular pieces of chalk or wooden pencils. Keep the points and edges sharp for accurate marking and use on the wrong side of the fabric.

Fade-away marker pens are air soluble and evaporate within forty-eight hours of use. Pens are easy to apply and the pointed tips allow for accurate marks. Whatever you choose, always test the marker on a piece of scrap fabric first.

Question 10:
Do I need an expensive sewing machine?

Choosing your very first sewing machine might seem a bit daunting, with so many different models on the market, and with prices ranging from fairly cheap—at just under $160—to pretty expensive—at well over $1,600. However, you should be able to buy a good-quality sewing machine that does all the stitches you will need for a reasonable price. It's also worth considering buying a secondhand sewing machine; aim to buy a reconditioned model and only opt for one that still comes with its instruction manual.

Before you buy, do some research into the different features offered by various machines. Online stores that give customer reviews are an ideal place to start. You will also find that department stores or larger sewing-supply shops that sell sewing machines will often have a particular salesperson who offers advice on all the different models. You can also usually get a free demonstration of those machines in which you are interested.

Some machines offer a myriad of different features and you may feel that you are getting so much more if you buy an expensive machine. However, you are often simply paying extra for additional decorative stitches that you won't really need for dressmaking. What is most important is the quality of the stitch and how easily the machine copes with multiple layers of fabric.

A good machine should include the following features: easy to thread; includes straight, zigzag, backstitch, and buttonhole stitches; an assortment of feet for different sewing tasks (see Question 12); a removable machine bed to enable easy sewing for cuffs and pants; a built-in light; and an instruction manual (particularly if buying secondhand).

ABOVE Modern sewing machines offer a range of different features. One that does straight, zigzag, backstitch, and buttonhole stitches will be ideal.

Question 11:
Do I need an overlocker?

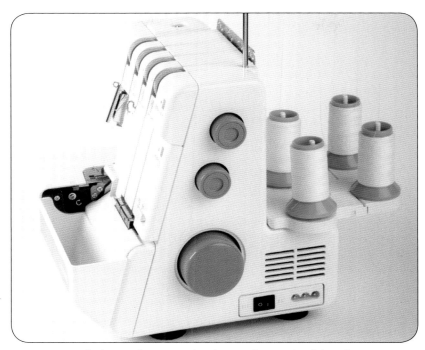

ABOVE An overlocker can be mounted with up to five spools of thread.

If you inspect the seams of most manufactured clothes they tend to be "overlocked." The exception to this is clothing made from some chiffon fabrics and the seams of jeans. With an overlocked seam, the machine used (an overlocker, also known as a serger) will stitch the seam, finish the raw edges, and cut off any excess fabric all in one step. If you are using an ordinary sewing machine, you would first stitch the seam before choosing a finishing method for the raw edges.

An overlocker generally uses three separate threads but it can have up to five. It may also feature decorative stitches. Although an overlocker is not essential for most domestic dressmaking, it is a fast and effective way of finishing off a garment professionally.

Question 12:
Which sewing machine accessories will I need?

Your sewing machine should come with a variety of accessories. The essentials are as follows.

• A straight-stitch foot: this is the sewing machine foot you need when working straight stitching and zigzag stitching.

• A zipper foot is used when sewing on zippers and piping, and when stitching bulky seams.

• A buttonhole sewing attachment measures the button and creates a buttonhole to exactly the right size. It does this all in one time-saving step. Most buttonhole attachments can also be adjusted manually if the button is too large to fit the slot. Always remember to make a test buttonhole on a scrap of fabric before embarking on stitching buttonholes on your garment.

Some machines come with additional accessories that are useful but not vital.

• An invisible-zipper foot is used when inserting an invisible zipper, the most desirable and effective zipper for skirts and dresses.

• A blind-hem foot allows you to hem using a sewing machine rather than by hand. When the hem is positioned correctly in the sewing machine, the needle and thread only catch up the fabric every few stitches to create a seemingly stitchless hem.

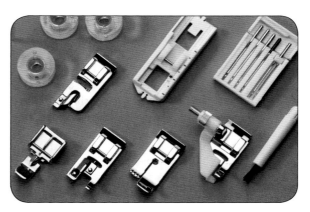

LEFT There are a variety of different accessories available for most sewing machines. Shown clockwise from top right are spare needles, a cleaning brush, blind-hem foot, straight-stitch foot, over-edge foot, zipper foot, spare bobbins, rolled-hem foot, buttonhole foot.

• An over-edge foot can finish seam edges and is an alternative to using an overlocker.

No sewing machine would be complete without the right needles and you need different needles for different fabrics. The needles you use depend on the type and weight of fabric you are sewing. For lightweight fabrics, such as chiffon or silk, use a fine needle, numbered 68/8. For mid-weight fabrics use a thicker needle, numbered 70/10 or 80/12; these are the sizes most commonly used in dressmaking. For heavier fabrics such as corduroy or denim, use a 90/14 needle. And for heavy-duty materials, such as upholstery fabric, use the thickest needle, numbered 100/16.

It's important to remember to change or discard needles regularly. With some fabrics, such as polyester, you may need to change needles two to three times since the material blunts the point easily.

Question 13:
How important is pressing?

Pressing is one of the most important procedures in making a garment. It is one of the key elements that will help you produce professional-looking clothes.

Using the tip of the iron makes pressing more responsive and enables easier access into small corners and tricky areas. After every seam has been stitched, take time to press it flat before going on to the next stage. Try not to stretch or pull the fabric when pressing, as with the use of steam this can sometimes permanently distort the fabric. Press on the wrong side of the fabric wherever possible especially when pressing seams, darts, and pleats.

Never press over pins. If the pin heads are plastic they may melt, and any pin will almost certainly leave an imprint on the fabric. Pins can also scratch the iron, which may in turn snag the fabric.

A pressing cloth is invaluable when pressing; it protects the fabric and eliminates any shine caused by ironing, especially on fabric that has a synthetic content. Use a square of clean cotton or muslin. Such a cloth is also essential when applying fusible interlining or interfacing, as the tacky substance that makes these fabrics fusible leaves a residue on the iron which can transfer to your newly pressed garment.

Question 14:
Will an ordinary iron and ironing board do?

Most households have an ordinary iron and ironing board for pressing and ironing clothes and this is perfectly adequate for dressmaking. However, it may be helpful to have an iron exclusively for sewing.

When purchasing a new iron for sewing think about choosing an iron that has steam on all settings. Steam is crucial when you're pressing, but not all fabrics can handle high temperatures so you need an iron that steams at lower temperature settings. Remember to empty the water tank after use as lime builds up quickly and a lime residue can be transferred onto your garment.

A tailors' ham is used for pressing darts, sleeve heads, and any rounded seams. It looks soft and rounded but it gives a firm and stable pressing surface. A sleeve board (which looks like a mini ironing board) is easier to use and a very handy addition to your pressing equipment. It is extremely useful for sleeves, necklines, and awkward seams.

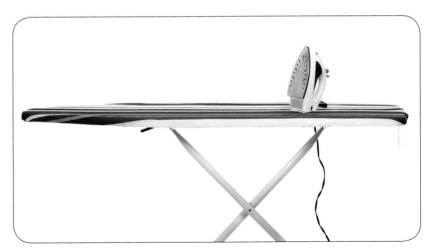

ABOVE An ordinary household ironing board will be adequate for most dressmaking. Do choose a good-quality iron that has variable steam settings.

Question 15:
How do I choose the right fabric?

There is a wide variety of fabrics from which to choose when it comes to selecting cloth for a garment and there seems to be two ways of deciding which fabric is right for you. If you have chosen the sewing pattern first, then this will dictate the type of fabric you need. If you have found a fabric you love, then you need to choose a sewing pattern to do it justice.

When choosing the fabric, consider what the garment is going to be used for, and bear in mind laundering, creasing, and how easy the fabric will be to make into a garment. There are a few "difficult" fabrics that require a level of experience, such as velvet (especially silk or viscose velvet) and chiffon, that might not be good choices for the beginner.

A commercial pattern gives you valuable information on the types of fabric suitable for that style. The reverse of the pattern envelope lists all the appropriate fabrics, their widths, and exactly how much fabric you need to buy.

It's worth remembering that large fabric prints work best on simple designs with few seams, such as a summer dress, loose skirt, or simple shirt. If you use a striped material, the stripes will need to match on the center front and sleeves.

EXPERT TIP

" Try to wrap the piece of fabric over yourself to get a feel of how the fabric drapes. A simple shift dress will look completely different depending on the fabric chosen: silk or synthetic crepe will hug your curves, whereas a cotton poplin or a silk dupion will give the dress a more structured look. "

ABOVE You'll find a wide range of different fabrics for sale in specialty fabric stores.

Question 16:
Do I choose natural or synthetic fabric?

Making a successful garment often depends on how easy it is to work with a fabric. You can toil away on a pair of pants made from an expensive polyester mix and struggle to get a professional finish. Whereas a hastily thrown together cotton summer skirt is a triumph.

Natural fabrics such as wool, cotton, and linen are all breathable and absorbent, making them comfortable to wear. Linen is a popular natural fabric made from the flax plant. The fabric is cool and absorbent and presses well when constructing. One of its characteristics is its tendency to crease, but it makes up easily into pants, shirts, skirts, and dresses. Check for laundering instructions when buying linen as sometimes manufacturers recommend dry cleaning.

Wool is naturally warm, wrinkle resistant, and absorbent. It is made from animal hair fibers, usually sheep, or goat if it's cashmere. Wool is easy to press and is made into dresses, skirts, pants, jackets, and coats. One hundred percent wool fabrics should be dry cleaned. Cotton is perhaps the most popular and commonly used fabric for

ABOVE Pure wool fabrics are warm and ideal for making jackets and coats. Wool mixed with a synthetic fiber has the advantage of being harder wearing.

dressmaking. Cotton is available as woven or knitted fabric. It can be bought in varying weights and is available in different textures and finishes. Characterized by its strength and durability, it is easy to press and is machine washable.

Over the past few years there have been many advances in fabric technology. Totally synthetic fabrics should be used with caution; they may be machine washable, drip dry, and crease resistant but they are difficult to work with. However, synthetic fibers work extremely well when mixed with either cotton, wool, or linen; they improve the natural fabrics and make them more crease resistant and washable.

Question 17:
Do I choose woven or knit fabrics?

When choosing a pattern the back of the envelope suggests fabrics suitable for the style and often it will stipulate whether it's suitable for woven or knit fabrics. It is advisable to adhere to the suggestions as knit patterns and woven patterns are quite different.

Patterns designed for knit fabrics have less moving room—known as "ease"—included, because there is enough stretch in the fabric.

This "ease" is included in patterns intended for woven fabrics, since these don't have as much give.

A woven fabric doesn't stretch and is made up of fibers running at 90-degree angles to each other. Knit fabrics are made up of interlocking loops of fiber that allow the fabric to stretch. The amount and direction of the stretch varies; a knit may stretch in one direction or in both.

ABOVE A woven material, made up of horizontal and vertical threads, will not have as much stretch in it as a knit fabric.

Question 18:
When should I choose jersey or other stretch fabrics?

Jersey or knit fabrics are comfortable to wear, drape well, and are generally crease resistant. They can be worn in almost all seasons. There are two types of knitted fabric. Weft knits are made by looping together continuous lengths of yarn. Made by hand or machine, weft knits stretch in one direction. Warp knits are made by loops of yarn that are interlocked vertically along the length of the fabric. This gives the material a two-way stretch and makes it ideal for swimwear and lingerie. Patterns meant for jersey or knit fabrics have fewer darts and seams as there is enough stretch in the fabric.

ABOVE A knit fabric is made up of interlocking loops of fiber and has a similar texture to fabric made by hand knitting.

Question 19:
Is it easy to use checked, plaid, or patterned fabrics?

A checked or plaid fabric can produce a dynamic, eye-catching garment, but if you pick a sewing pattern not specifically designed for these fabrics, problems will arise. Such fabrics must be matched at seams and style lines if the garment is going to look attractive. Try to find a pattern that has only a few simple seams and not too much detailing. Eased seams, bias seams, or a large number of pattern pieces will add to your matching problems.

It is not possible to match the check on every seam so before you start decide on which seams to concentrate. Before cutting anything, spend a little time laying out the pattern pieces on the fabric and mark any plaid points on the pattern with a soft pencil.

For a good visual effect, there are a few key areas to remember when matching check or plaid fabric. Try to have the middle of the check on the center front—this is usually where the button placement is—and not at the edge of the pattern. Choose a check line to continue from the chest area through to the sleeves. The center of the check

ABOVE Whatever plaid you choose—this one's Royal Stewart—take care when matching the pattern at any garment seams.

should run down the middle of the sleeve and match horizontally with a check running from the chest area. Choose the middle of a check for the center back and remember when matching checks to allow for the seam allowances.

Patterned fabrics are easier to work with than checks but a few rules still apply. Again, choose sewing patterns with few seams and style lines. Lay your pattern pieces on the fabric in the same direction, unless you know the design works both up and down the fabric.

Question 20:
I've been given some silk; what could I make out of it?

Silk is made from natural fibers of the unwound cocoon of the silkworm. It is a very comfortable fabric to wear with high absorbency characteristics, making it cool in warm weather. And because it is a fiber that has a low conductivity, it keeps warm air close to the skin during cold weather.

Silk comes in a variety of weights and weaves but, generally speaking, it's a lightweight fabric that's commonly used for shirts, blouses, pajamas, sun dresses, and lingerie. There are a number of types of silk, such as slub or raw, habotai, organza, faille, ottoman, and damask. Among the more well-known varieties are silk crepe de chine, a lightweight plain-weave silk with a soft feel that lends itself to unstructured shapes with gathers and pleats, such as simple blouses, floaty skirts, sun dresses, or lingerie. Dupion silk is a luxurious heavier fabric, usually in beautiful jewel colors and with a slightly papery texture; it's used for formal dresses, bridal gowns, and jackets. Silk chiffon, or georgette, is a fine sheer fabric with a soft handle, often used as an overlay over another fabric in a skirt or dress; avoid using it in tight-fitting styles with darts and seams.

ABOVE Silk is a beautiful, flowing fabric and comes in a huge range of colors and weights, from ultralight organza through to heavier crepe de chine.

Essential Equipment and Choosing Fabric

Question 21:
What should I use for lining?

ABOVE In lightweight garments you should choose a lining that is a near color match, but in a heavier weight garment, you could pick a strongly contrasting color.

Lining has several functions in a garment. It adds comfort and warmth, and it helps to preserve the shape of the garment by preventing stretching and wrinkling.

A lining is assembled separately and placed wrong side to wrong side of the garment. It gives a perfectly smooth finish inside.

Normally the lining is a satin fabric with a slippery surface, so the garment is easy to get on and off. Synthetic satin linings are available in various weights and are perfect for lining jackets, skirts, and winter dresses. If you need to line a garment that will be worn in warmer weather, choose a silk lining so it will be cooler and more breathable next to the skin.

When choosing a lining, check that the laundering instructions are compatible with the fabric of the main garment. There is no point having a dry-clean-only lining inside a machine-washable dress.

Question 22:
What sort of interlining should I use?

Interlining—which is sometimes referred to as interfacing, fusing, or Vilene—is used to give shape and support to garments. It is usually used on collars, waistbands, facings, and cuffs. Horsehair canvas is still hand sewn into custom-made tailored jackets but nowadays, fusible interfacing—either woven or bonded—is found in virtually all garments. Interlining is available in various weights and is backed with a heat-fusing film. It is cut to size and placed on the wrong side of the fabric, covered with a press cloth, and ironed.

Use a hot iron with steam when fusing to make sure it has completely stuck to the fabric. If you find bubbles in the interlining, it hasn't been properly applied and will detach itself from the fabric when washed. The fashion industry uses ironing boards with a built-in vacuum; the suction helps the fusing to bond fully. It is worthwhile fusing a piece of interlining onto a scrap of your chosen fabric to test that the result is as stiff as you would like; it can be hard to tell how the interlining will perform before it has been fused.

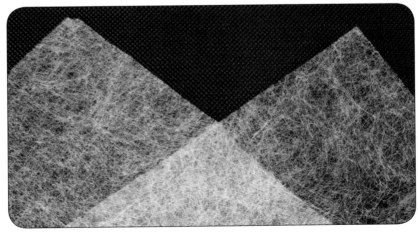

ABOVE Fusible interlining comes in a variety of weights. The finest variety is so lightweight as to be almost transparent.

Question 23:
Which threads should I choose?

A large range of thread is available and your choice depends on what you are making and whether it's for hand stitching or machine sewing. It's easy to become confused by the choices available, but for a general-purpose thread for use on your sewing machine, either polyester or mercerized cotton is appropriate. Both the polyester and cotton are available in large cones, suitable for an overlocker.

You can also buy a basting thread that is ideal for temporary stitching like tacking or tailor's tacks. When time is short, this thread is easily broken by your fingers.

Topstitching thread is a stronger, thicker thread that gives a bolder, decorative finish. It is also used for hand sewing buttonholes. On your sewing machine you need to fit a needle with a larger eye to carry the thickness of thread with a general-purpose thread wound onto the bobbin.

I have only discussed a few thread options but the range is limitless with silk, metallic, and nylon threads available.

LEFT There's a color of thread suitable for every project. If you can't find an exact match, always choose a thread that's a slightly darker shade than the fabric.

Question 24:
What sort of buttons and other fasteners should I choose?

Buttons can be made out of plastic, shell, horn, and metal, or they can be covered with fabric. They can be sewn onto clothing either by stitching through holes in the button, or by stitching through a loop (known as the shank) on the underside of the button.

When choosing buttons for your garments the first thing to check is that you can make a large enough—or small enough—buttonhole with your sewing machine. The next thing to consider is whether the buttons are a suitable weight for the fabric you are using; a big heavy button will drag a lightweight fabric out of shape, and a small flimsy button won't hold together layers of thick, heavyweight fabric. You should also check that the buttons match up with the care needs of your chosen fabric; if your fabric is machine washable or dry-clean only, then you need to be able to do the same with the buttons.

There are other means to secure closures but these are generally hidden and play no additional decorative role in a garment. At waistbands, it's common to use a

hook-and-eye style fastening or a snap fastener. Velcro is also handy on any overlapping opening in clothing, particularly where there is not much stress placed on the opening and it's less likely to be pulled apart during wear. And of course there are zippers, invaluable closures for so many different garments, at the waists of pants and skirts in particular.

ABOVE Buttons are stitched on through holes—they have two or four holes—or through a loop on the back of the button, called the shank.

Question 25:
What sort of zipper should I use?

ABOVE With a wide range of colors available, there's a zipper to match any fabric.

A zipper is made of two sets of interlocking teeth, each attached to a strip of fabric tape; a slider is pulled along the teeth to draw them together or pull them apart. Zippers can be made out of metal, nylon, or plastic, and are available in various different lengths and colors.

The invisible or concealed zipper is a lightweight zipper commonly used when an elegant finish is required on a garment. This type is very easy to insert and can be used on dresses, tops, skirts, and pants. It's available in many different lengths, but if you can't find the exact length required, the beauty of this zipper is that it may be cut to size. Available in various colors the zipper is completely covered by the fabric when inserted, with the only

exposed area being the slider pull. So although it will be worth getting a similar color of zipper, a perfect match is not essential.

The conventional zipper is available in many lengths and a vast selection of colors. This is a robust zipper suitable for pants and hard-wearing garments. There are several ways of inserting this type of zipper. Probably the most common technique is the lapped method, where a flap of fabric covers the zipper, as is commonly found in jeans. The open-ended zipper can be undone from either the top or bottom and it is often made from metal or heavy-duty plastic. It's used on jackets and other outerwear where it is necessary to be able to undo the zipper from both top and bottom.

26 How do I know which body shape I am?

27 What clothing styles will best suit my body shape?

28 What do I get if I buy a commercial sewing pattern?

29 Where can I buy commercial patterns?

30 Can I download sewing patterns from the Internet?

31 How do I know how difficult the pattern is?

32 How do I buy the right pattern for my size?

33 How do I understand the back of the envelope?

34 How do I know how much fabric to buy?

35 What is meant by lining, interlining, and interfacing?

36 What are notions?

37 What does the information sheet tell me?

38 What does the pattern terminology mean?

39 What do the layout plans mean?

40 What do the numbers printed on the pattern pieces indicate?

41 What do the different dotted lines around the edge of the pattern pieces mean?

42 There are triangle shapes printed on the pattern; what are these?

43 What do the small circles indicate?

44 There's a long line with an arrow at the end on each piece; what is this?

2

CHOOSING AND UNDERSTANDING PATTERNS

Question 26:
How do I know which body shape I am?

One of the great advantages of making your own clothes is being able to adjust patterns to suit your particular body shape so that you no longer have to put up with garments that don't quite fit. There are some basic body-shape classifications and descriptions that can help you to achieve a style best suited to your figure. Depending on the manufacturer of the pattern you choose, there is often a silhouette key on the back of the pattern envelope which indicates the body shape that pattern is recommended for. There are many variations on these fundamental body shapes, but fashion and styling becomes easier if you know into which basic category you fit.

- The most common body shape is the rectangle. With very few obvious curves, a rectangular figure will have no defined waist. People with rectangular body shapes often find they need tall or petite sizes when buying ready-made clothes.

- The hourglass shape is often regarded as the ideal body shape. It has a visibly nipped-in waist, and the hips and shoulders are balanced in line with one another. If you have an hourglass shape, you will usually find when buying clothes that you are the same dress size top and bottom.

- The pear shape, or bottom-heavy triangle, is noticeable in that the shoulders are narrower in relation to the hips and lower body. Pear shapes are likely to find that they need to buy pants that are one or even two sizes larger than their top size.

- The top-heavy triangle shape is when the upper body is broad across the shoulders and with a big bust. People with this body shape will generally find they need a larger size on the top than the bottom.

- The circle shape will have a large frame with a prominent tummy, along with sloping shoulders, a wide hipline and, more than likely, an ample bust.

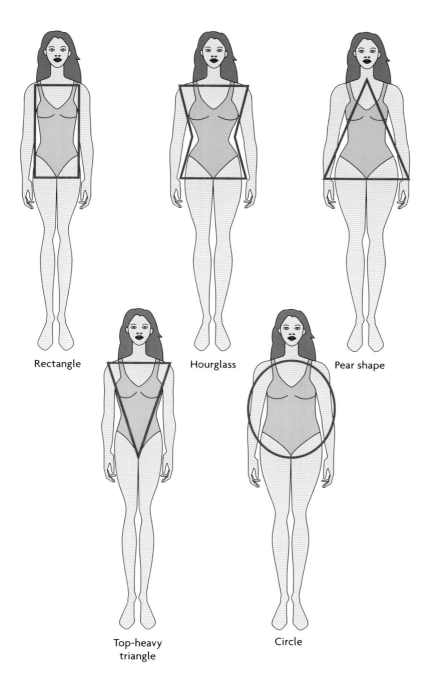

Rectangle   Hourglass   Pear shape

Top-heavy
triangle

Circle

Question 27:
What clothing styles will best suit my body shape?

Having thought about your body shape and looked through your wardrobe, there will undoubtedly be a common theme to the styles you normally choose to wear. When making your own clothes, however, it's often easy to forget what suits your figure type as you don't have the chance to try on the garments before you decide. Here are a few pointers to remember when picking out styles in the pattern book.

- Anyone with a rectangle body shape should look for A-line or flared skirts and tops that have some style detail at the bust. This will give the illusion of more prominent bust and hips.
- Hourglass shapes will find that "V" necklines in softly styled tops that drape over the body work well when teamed with pencil skirts that emphasize the waistline. Wraparound shirts and dresses in jersey knits as well as any bias-cut styles will also enhance an hourglass figure.
- A pear shape, however, wants to focus attention on her waist and so should go for belted styles, as well as tops with cowl necklines or any other detailing that gives the illusion of a wider top half. Pants without pleats in plain fabrics are flattering.
- Top-heavy triangle body types look good above the waist in simple, smooth, clean lines in plain or small prints. Team these with tailored, wide-legged pants to balance out the silhouette.
- One of the hardest figure types to dress is the circle (sometimes known as the apple shape). The aim is to define the waist as much as possible and wearing tummy control underwear is a start. Using decorative necklines will draw the eye up and away from the waist as well as using prints and patterns to draw the eye away from the body. Wearing shorter skirts and dresses in soft fabrics gives the appearance of a longer body.

ABOVE If you have a circle body shape, choose a dress style that draws the eye toward the neckline and that emphasizes the waistline.

Question 28:
What do I get if I buy a commercial sewing pattern?

Commercial patterns are printed on tissue paper and sold in packets. Patterns are available in a wide range of sizes, styles, prices, and sewing skill levels.

When buying a pattern it usually includes more than one size, which helps when you need to adapt a pattern to your figure type. The front of the envelope gives multiple views of the garment. It may show style differences and length variations. The back of the envelope provides a guide to sizing, fabric suitability and the amounts needed, and the fastenings and trimmings required. Inside the envelope there is a detailed information sheet that includes fabric layouts and instructions on making the garment.

Question 29:
Where can I buy commercial patterns?

Most shops that sell dressmaking fabrics will have sewing pattern catalogues from the main manufacturers. You simply go through the catalogue and select the pattern you want.

Buying a pattern online is also an option. The big pattern companies have their own websites and you will also find other retailers that offer a selection from several different pattern companies.

Once you have made a few garments using different pattern companies, you may discover favorites, possibly because their fit suits you best, or because you like their instruction style. Vogue patterns tend to be more expensive, but they do offer designer fashions. Butterick's and McCall's patterns are more mainstream in their look. Simplicity, New Look, and Kwik Sew make good basic patterns and Burda offers interesting fashions, although their patterns require a little more experience as they sometimes come without seam allowances.

Question 30:
Can I download sewing patterns from the Internet?

Downloading patterns is becoming more popular as technology is improving all the time and provides an easier option if you urgently want a pattern and getting to a fabric shop is difficult. There is no postage to pay when buying a pattern online so a download can be a cheaper way to purchasing a style. Many sites have frequent sales and some sites even offer various patterns free. Many companies have chat rooms where home sewers can exchange sewing experiences with each other, along with photos of their completed projects.

When downloading a pattern it is split into 8-½ x 11 inch page sizes so it can be used with a standard home printer. The pages then need to be stuck together before being cut into the pattern pieces. This is a fairly lengthy process, especially for the more complicated designs, so it does take time and patience. However, once you have downloaded a pattern you can print off as many copies as you want, which is a great benefit if you are making multiple sizes of one design, or if you make a mistake when cutting out a pattern piece!

ABOVE Downloaded patterns feature special guide marks and trim lines to make it easier for you to assemble the pattern once printed out.

Question 31:
How do I know how difficult the pattern is?

Most pattern companies mark the level of difficulty on the front of the pattern. The simplest patterns are usually marked as "very easy" or "easy" and then progress to "average" and "advanced."

Depending on your ability, your experience working with patterns, and how confident you feel, choose a sewing pattern that is equal to your skill level as you are more likely to be pleased with the finished clothes. It's better to choose a simple design and produce a well-made garment than risk being frustrated and not finishing a complicated item.

The pattern envelope is full of information that at first glance can appear daunting. If the envelope doesn't specify what skill level is necessary, then check the information sheet inside to see how many pattern pieces are needed to complete the garment; if you carefully follow the step-by-step instructions on the sheet, then making the garment is not dissimilar to following a recipe. Generally speaking, the more pieces there are, the longer it will take to make the garment. Often the skill level suggested on the pattern envelope will be because certain skills are needed; for example, to insert a zipper, to make buttonholes, or to understand style details such as pleats on the garment.

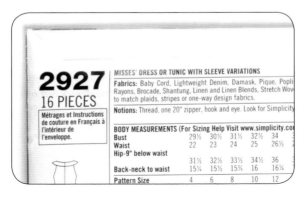

LEFT If the skill level isn't given on a pattern, look for the number of pieces it contains. As a rule of thumb, the more pieces there are, the more complex the pattern will be to construct.

Question 32:
How do I buy the right pattern for my size?

On the back of the pattern envelope you will find imperial and metric body measurements as well as a size chart. Commercial patterns are often sold with two to three sizes on one pattern, such as sizes 10, 12, and 14. It is best to know your basic body measurements (bust, waist, and hips) before buying a pattern, as this will guide you to the appropriate size; see the questions in Chapter 3 for more information on taking the right measurements. Don't be alarmed if the size you appear to be on the back of the pattern envelope doesn't compare to your normal ready-to-wear clothing size; sewing patterns are generally larger. And don't worry if you are a plus size; many pattern manufacturers offer patterns in larger sizes and you can follow the instructions in this book to alter these to suit your own particular body shape.

When comparing measurements for each size, it is unlikely that all your measurements will be exactly one size—your bust may be a size 12, for example, but your hips may be a size 14. Remember when buying a pattern for pants or a skirt to choose the pattern size by your hip measurement, and when buying a pattern for a jacket, top, or dress, choose the pattern size based on your bust measurement. If your actual measurements fall between two sizes, generally go for the larger size as it can then be adjusted. Multisize patterns are handy if your measurements are very different from the standard size; for example, if you have large hips and a small waist, the pattern can be altered to fit.

EXPERT TIP

66 Write your measurements on a card and keep it in your purse. When shopping for a pattern, you will have them on hand and this takes the guesswork out of choosing the right size. 99

Question 33:
How do I understand the back of the envelope?

On the back of the pattern envelope you will find a lot of different information. This can seem daunting at first glance but when broken down into the different elements you will see that it gives you essential information about the garment, as well as a note as to what you may need to purchase while still in the fabric shop.

First, there is a style number, which may be just a number or a combination of letters and numbers, depending on the pattern manufacturer. Then you will find a description of the garment, with information such as how fitted it is, what the length of the style is, whether it's lined or interlined, and what sort of fastenings it has. A list of suggested fabrics for the pattern follows, which may also include a list of unsuitable options; this is worth taking note of, as the correct fabric choice is crucial for a successful creation.

Notions are listed, so read carefully and purchase what is needed to complete the project, as it's easier to match zippers, buttons, seam binding, or elastic while you have all the fabric in front of you.

There are detailed diagrams of the styles, showing the front and back views, generally marked A, B, C, and D, depending on how many designs the pattern contains. A guide is included to help you calculate how much fabric, lining, and interfacing you will need to buy.

As well as the measurement guide to sizes, there are also some finished garment measurements; for instance, waist to hem on pants and skirts.

EXPERT TIP

❝ It's worth marking your chosen style in the fabric calculations column on the back of the envelope. When you're in a busy fabric shop it's easy to confuse the different columns and end up buying the wrong amount of fabric. ❞

BELOW At the top left of this pattern envelope, you will see a four-digit number; this is the style number (1). Just below, the number of pattern pieces are indicated (2), with diagrams of the different styles (3) you can make from the one pattern. Many patterns are sold in several different countries so you will often find the envelope features information in English and another language; here, the information is divided into two columns, English on the left and French on the right.

At the top is the name of the style followed by a list of suitable fabrics and the notions you will need to buy (4). Below this you'll find the body measurements used by the pattern company and the sizes that they correspond to (5). A guide to the amount of fabric you will need follows, including linings and interfacings (6). There is also information on special notions that you might include to add a "designer touch" to the finished garment. At the bottom you will find a table of the finished measurements of the garment (7). This includes the "ease"; see Question 56.

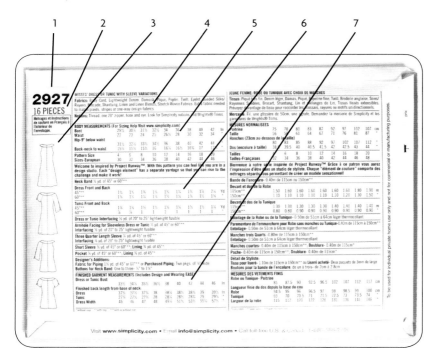

Question 34:
How do I know how much fabric to buy?

On the back of the pattern envelope, a fabric calculations section is included to tell you how much fabric, notions, and lining are needed. Depending on how wide the fabric is on the roll will determine how much fabric is needed. It's not a hard-and-fast rule, but fabric is generally manufactured in widths of either 45 inches (115 cm) or 60 inches (150 cm). The pattern envelope will list fabric requirements for specific widths.

Fabrics with a one-way print or a nap (such as velvet or corduroy) will require more fabric, since the pattern pieces have to be placed on to the fabric in one direction only. Velvet and corduroy will have a shaded appearance if cut "up and down" the fabric. Allow more material to match plaids, other checks, and large diagonals.

Commercial patterns are usually generous with fabric calculations to allow for size ranges and error.

Question 35:
What is meant by lining, interlining, and interfacing?

To make a successful garment that has shape, durability, and continues to look good when cleaned requires a certain amount of support within the garment. Lining, interlining, and interfacing are integral parts of the garment that generally go unseen but serve an important function in maintaining the shape and comfort of your creation.

A lining helps hide the inner construction of a garment, as well as providing a surface that allows the garment to slide on and over other clothing easily. Lining fabrics are usually slippery and silky and are often made out of synthetic material. The lining is constructed separately from the garment and attached at the hem areas and facings by hand or machine.

There are two forms of interlining. One is when fabric is added to a garment where more warmth is needed, in a winter coat, for example. It's made separately, then attached, and may be removable. The other meaning of interlining is when two fabrics are put together as if only one layer, such as a canvas inside a man's wool jacket or a silk organza underneath the satin of a wedding dress. This is done to give structure and body to the main fabric.

Interfacing, like interlining, is a support fabric used in areas that require more stability; generally collars, cuffs, waistbands, facings, and sometimes hems. It is available in white and various shades of gray in differing weights. There is a fusible variety, with an adhesive on one side that is pressed on with an iron. The other variety looks the same as the fusible but is sewn in.

Question 36:
What are notions?

Notions is collective term for a variety of small objects or accessories. Notions can include items that are sewn or otherwise attached to a finished garment, such as buttons, snaps, zippers, and shoulder pads, but the term also includes small tools used in sewing such as thread, pins,

marking pens, and seam rippers.

Once you have chosen a pattern and some fabric, this is the time to purchase all the extras you need to make your garment. You will probably find all you need in your local fabric shop but there are many wonderful shops selling special and unusual notions.

ABOVE Ribbons and other decorative trims come under the heading of notions.

Question 37:
What does the information sheet tell me?

The information sheet is enclosed in the envelope with the pattern. This sheet provides information and step-by-step instructions on how to make your garment.

Diagrams of the styles, marked with their letters, are shown as well as a breakdown of which pattern piece is needed for your chosen style. A body-measurement chart is included on the sheet along with a key to pattern terminology. Also shown on the sheet are suggested cutting layouts for your fabric width; check carefully for the correct layout for your selected style. There may also be layouts for interfacing and interlining. It helps

EXPERT TIP

66 Put each pattern piece required to make your style to one side and fold all the other unwanted pieces and return to the envelope. It helps to eliminate any possible confusion later. 99

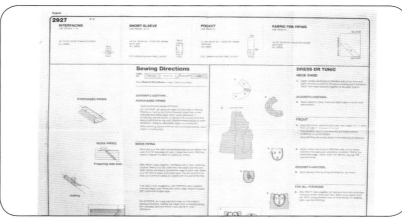

ABOVE You'll find instructions for all parts of the garment construction on the information sheet.

to highlight the correct layouts for your chosen style as this will enable you to stay focused on the right part of the information sheet.

Depending on how complicated the design is, there are normally two sheets enclosed with the pattern: one is the information sheet, the other is the instructions on how to construct the garment. Ideally, you should read through both before you even cut out the pattern in order to familiarize yourself with the process.

Question 38:
What does the pattern terminology mean?

Pattern terminology consists of the technical terms used in dressmaking and the fashion industry. The information sheet enclosed with a commercial sewing pattern will have a key to the pattern terminology used to help the maker understand the instructions and construct the garment. It takes a little time for the terminology to be comprehensible but once you have made a couple of styles it will become clearer.

First, the information sheet will tell you about the seam allowances; it's always worth checking this as pattern companies vary. Other information concerns where to place the pattern on the fabric, which way to fold the fabric before cutting, and whether single- or double-thickness fabric is needed in certain parts of the pattern.

The information sheet tells you to transfer all markings from the pattern to the fabric; this includes notches, tailor's tacks, darts, and anything that may help you construct the garment.

Often in the step-by-step instructions it will tell you to baste or tack an area together. This is the term for temporary stitching, usually in a different color thread, that is used to hold pieces of fabric in place and which is then removed when permanent sewing is done. Another term referred to in commercial patterns is stay-stitching. This is a line of stitching just inside the intended stitching line (the seam line) used on curved edges to help stabilize and keep the curve from distorting; for example, on necklines, shoulders, and armholes.

Question 39:
What do the layout plans mean?

The layout is a term that describes a way of placing all the pattern pieces for your style in an economical manner on the fabric. There are several different layout plans on the information sheet, each determined by the fabric width, as well as plans for lining and interfacing.

When you have found and marked the correct layout for your style, look at how the pattern pieces have been placed in the diagram. The layout is shown with the fabric folded, so when you cut a sleeve, for example, you are actually cutting a pair. If asked to place a pattern on the fold (see Question 78) then only a single piece is required such as the front of a dress.

On the layout plan, some pieces are shaded: this indicates the right side of the fabric; the lighter pieces indicate the wrong side.

It's worthwhile spending time laying out your pattern on the fabric to make sure you are cutting out all the pieces you need. Allow ¾–1¼ inches (2–3 cm) between pattern pieces and don't worry too much if you need to cut a new set of cuffs or a collar; commercial patterns are quite generous with the fabric needed and there is usually room to recut for a small mistake.

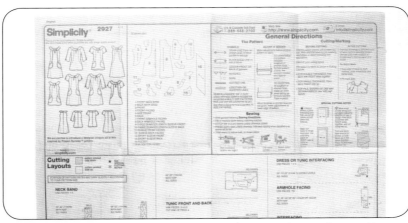

ABOVE The heading "Cutting Layouts" indicates the various layout plans on this information sheet.

Question 40:
What do the numbers printed on the pattern pieces indicate?

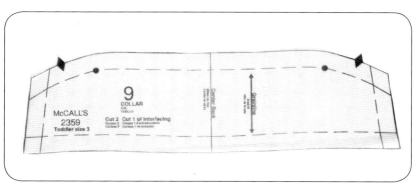

ABOVE A pattern piece is identified by the name of the part—in this case, a collar—and this is given a number—here it's 9—that corresponds to the layout plan.

The style option you have chosen from your sewing pattern will be made up of a number of pieces; all of them will have numbers printed on them. This essential bit of information helps you to work out what you need from the mass of tissue paper that you'll find when you undo your neatly folded commercial pattern; a mass of tissue paper that never seems to fold back neatly into the envelope!

On each pattern piece you will find the name of the company, style number, the number that identifies the pattern piece, its name, and the number of fabric pieces to cut. You will also find out if the piece is to be cut out of the main fabric and/ or the lining or interfacing. All the information on the pattern should enable you to lay out the pattern and cut the fabric even if you have mislaid the information sheet.

The information you find on a pattern is even more crucial as you start to become more confident and combine patterns, adding a sleeve or pocket from another garment, for example. Try to keep pattern pieces in their original envelopes. It's very easy to get the pieces muddled up and mislaid in other envelopes.

Question 41:
What do the different dotted lines around the edge of the pattern pieces mean?

Having laid out your pattern you will notice that there are three or four different dotted lines around the edge of the pattern pieces, ranging from small dots to one continuous line. The continuous black line marks the cutting line but be careful anywhere with a dotted line, as this usually indicates a different size.

Once you have decided what size you want, look at the pattern carefully. The main size lines around the pattern are fairly easy to work out but take care to find the correct size for darts, waist area, pockets, and other details. It can be helpful to use a highlighter and mark every area on the pattern where your size appears.

After you have checked that you have the right size and line, cut out the pattern. Make sure you cut outside the line, and be as accurate as possible.

ABOVE Trim along the dotted line which corresponds to your size.

EXPERT TIP

❝ You may want to make several sizes from one pattern—to make three or four bridesmaids' dresses, for example—and don't want to cut the pattern to the smallest size. The quick solution is to just fold away the bigger sizes. However, on some areas, like the waist and armhole curves, you may need to snip into the pattern to fold it away. This makes the pattern a bit fragile when you come to unfold it for the larger sizes. Run masking tape over the area near the edges and then do your cutting. You will have a stronger pattern edge that will survive longer. ❞

Question 42:
There are triangle shapes printed on the pattern; what are these?

On the pattern you will see a series of single and double triangle shapes scattered around the pattern pieces. In fact, virtually every piece will have at least one and at the sleeve and armhole there will be several. These triangles are called notches and are symbols for matching seams. Such markings are vital for transferring information from the pattern to the fabric and enable the maker to successfully make a garment. Not only do the notches mark the seams but they also mark the front and back of the sleeve, as well as design details such as darts and where the zipper will stop. If the notches are not put on to the fabric, it's virtually impossible to produce a perfect pair of sleeves set into an armhole with the correct pitch.

Often on commercial patterns the instructions suggest when cutting out the pattern with the fabric, to cut the notches in a little extra piece out of the pattern area; this is a fairly tricky process. In the fashion industry notches are carefully snipped into the seam allowance by about ¼ inches (5 mm) which is faster and more accurate.

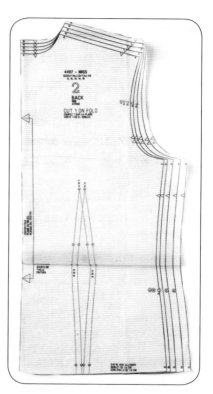

ABOVE Notches are indicated by small triangles printed on the pattern.

Question 43:
What do the small circles indicate?

As with the notches, you will see small circles dotted over most of the pattern pieces. These indicate a "matching point" that will correspond to another matching point on either the same pattern piece or an adjacent piece.

On commercial patterns the suggested way of marking these circles is by using tailor's tacks. The tailor's tack is essentially two threads in a needle preferably in a contrasting color, drawn through fabric in one or more layers and then snipped leaving the tails of thread on top and on the bottom of the fabric as a marking for later use. The tailor's tack is used to mark darts, buttonhole positions, pocket positions, and other details that will help with garment construction.

In the fashion industry, with the exception of haute couture design houses, there is no time to do tailor's tacks, so important points on the pattern such as darts are marked with a small hole.

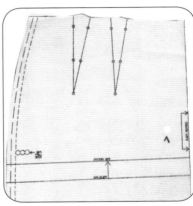

ABOVE By matching up the small circles on the darts shown above, you will get a better fit at the waist of this skirt.

Question 44:
There's a long line with an arrow at the end on each piece; what is this?

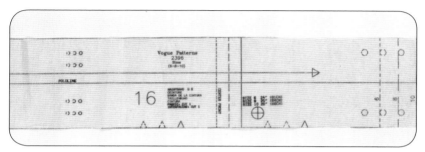

ABOVE The long arrow indicates where to match a pattern piece to the grain.

The symbol that looks like a long arrow on every pattern piece indicates how the pattern should match the fabric's grain line. The arrow at one end points in the direction of the pile when using fabric with a nap (velvet or corduroy) with the smooth or right side of the fabric running in the direction of the arrow.

Have you ever had a pair of jeans that wanted to twist around your legs when you walked, or a t-shirt with a side seam that constantly swings toward the back? If so, this is because the garments were cut "off the grain" and generally happens in cheap clothing.

The grain line controls how fabric hangs, whether it's on your body or as curtains. It's important to make sure the pattern piece is placed on the fabric with the grain line parallel to the selvedge; this is done by measuring from the selvedge to the grain line marking on the pattern. To find out more about the grain line see Questions 70 and 77.

45 What are the essential body measurements for determining my size?

46 What is a good fit?

47 I am tall and most patterns don't fit; what are the key areas to adjust?

48 I am short and feel swamped by most patterns; what are the key areas to adjust?

49 How do I take my measurements accurately?

50 How do I take a bust measurement?

51 How do I take a waist measurement?

52 How do I take a hip measurement?

53 How do I take a back-neck to waist measurement?

54 How do I take a sleeve measurement?

55 What other aspects of my body shape should I take into consideration?

56 What is "tolerance" or "ease"?

57 Can I adapt a tailor's dummy to my size?

58 Is it worth making a "toile" or tester garment?

59 What fabric should I use to make the toile?

60 How do I make the toile?

61 When I try on the toile, how do I know if it's a good fit?

62 Before I start, is there a sequence for pattern alterations?

63 How do I know what seam allowances there are?

64 How do I measure the pattern?

3

TAKING MEASUREMENTS AND GETTING A GOOD FIT

Question 45:
What are the essential body measurements for determining my size?

When buying a sewing pattern it's important to be realistic about the size you are. People often measure themselves and then still don't buy the right size, thinking they are not that big. The confusion arises since sewing pattern sizes seem to be larger than store-bought clothes.

Clothing is designed to fit your shoulders and flow smoothly over your figure and to produce a nicely fitting garment, so it's important to take accurate measurements.

There are plenty of useful measurements to take when making a garment but to purchase a pattern there are only a few essential dimensions that determine what standard size you are. They are the bust, waist, hip, and back-neck to waist. See Questions 49 to 54 for more information.

Question 46:
What is a good fit?

Good-fitting clothing should be a blend of two elements: how the garment looks and how comfortable it is to wear. How you view a good fit varies depending on different body shapes but to establish whether a garment fits there are a few essentials.

In any piece of clothing there are several key comfort areas, such as the armholes and neckline. If you can feel any points rubbing or catching, then the armhole may be too high under the arm or the neckline too tight.

When trying on a suit, for example, check that the dress sits well underneath the jacket, the neckline is lying flat against the body, and there are no wrinkles or creases appearing around the bust area. Make sure you are able to raise your arms comfortably without straining. The jacket should sit easily around the waist and the buttons should be easy to fasten.

ABOVE A good fit isn't just about how a garment looks in the mirror. Make sure you move around and try sitting in an outfit to see if it's completely comfortable.

Question 47:
I am tall and most patterns don't fit; what are the key areas to adjust?

The obvious problems that tall people find when trying on clothes are that pants and sleeves tend to be too short. However, the back-neck to waist measurement is often too short as well. This can mean that the waistline on dresses and jackets sits above the natural waistline, which in turn makes the hip area feel tight on fitted dresses. Tall women often find buying a dress very frustrating and opt for a skirt and top instead.

The back-neck to waist measurement is easily altered on a commercial pattern by cutting through the adjustment line that runs across the waist areas on all pattern pieces. Once you have cut through the line you can extend the pattern to your measurement by adding in a piece of paper. Remember to alter all the relevant pattern pieces and to redraw a smooth cutting line over the attached paper extension.

The sleeve and armhole area on a top may also feel tight on tall people, as the measurement between the shoulder and the bottom of the armhole is often too short on the pattern. This can be altered by adding to the armhole area on the bodice and by increasing the sleeve head by a corresponding amount—see Question 129. If your pattern has a side front panel and a side back panel and you don't draw the line through them, they won't have to be altered.

When altering the back-neck and armhole areas, remember to disperse any added measurement between the two points to create a balanced garment.

Question 48:
I am short and feel swamped by most patterns; what are the key areas to adjust?

One of the telltale signs of being swamped by clothing is an extra wrinkle or fold of fabric sitting just above the waist or too much fabric between the armhole and the neck.

This problem arises if the back-neck to waist measurement is shorter than the average. Once a garment has been made, it's impossible to rectify a back-neck to waist that hasn't been altered to fit the person. You can alter sleeve length, hems, and take in at the seams but not the back-neck to waist. Patterns have a lengthening and shortening line marked on or just above the waist and this can easily be adjusted by folding a section out of the pattern once you know your back-neck to waist measurement (see Question 53).

The other problem for a petite person is the area between the armhole and neck; necklines can appear to bulge, and lapel and jacket fronts won't sit flat on the body. Some commercial patterns have an adjustment line that runs through the sleeve to the armhole, as well as through the back and front bodices to the armhole. The same amount has to be folded out of the pattern on the sleeve, and the front and back bodices.

Once you have your back-neck to waist measurement, you want to divide the amount you want to take out between the key areas to adjust. If, for example, your measurement is 1¼ inches (3 cm) shorter than the pattern, it would be best to take out half of this measurement through the waist and half through the sleeve and bodice. It is better to disperse the amount you want to take out, rather than try and eliminate a large chunk from one area.

If you know you are a very small size, it is well worth making a "toile" or a tester garment before you alter the pattern (see Question 60). It's faster to make than you think and you can see where the extra fabric needs taking out.

Question 49:
How do I take my measurements accurately?

To select a sewing pattern you need to know your measurements to make sense of the size charts. It's important to take a bit of time to do the measuring properly. Get measured wearing a good-fitting bra that supports your bust properly; the difference in appearance when fitting a dress or top with decent undergarments is phenomenal.

First of all, find a friend who is willing to help as it's practically impossible to succeed alone. Stand with feet and legs together, back straight, and look straight ahead. Shoulders should be relaxed with arms by your side. Use a tape measure and keep it taut. Don't pull it too tight, however, when measuring around the waist or hips.

Keep a record of your measurements and remeasure every six months or so to keep it up to date. Take a photocopy of the chart below and then fill it in with your measurements as you take them. When buying a pattern, write the pattern measurements in the relevant column and then work out the difference between the two. This will help you decide which size pattern to buy and indicate where and by how much you need to alter a pattern.

Measurement position	Your measurement	The pattern measurement	The difference between the two
Bust			
Waist			
Hip			
Back-neck to waist			
Sleeve			

Question 50:
How do I take a bust measurement?

To take an accurate bust measurement, wear an unpadded bra and place the tape measure under your arms and wrap around the fullest area of the bust. Make sure your arms are down at your sides and the tape measure is horizontal and not slipping at the back. Take the measurement keeping the tape snug on the body.

If you would like to find your bra size, write down the measurement you've just taken, rounding up any fractional measurements to the nearest whole number. To find your band or under-bust measurement, measure directly under your bust after expelling all air from your lungs—you want this measurement to be as small as possible. Again, round up any fractional numbers. If the measurement is even, add 4 inches (10 cm) and if it's odd, add 5 inches (12.5 cm). Finally, to calculate your bra size, subtract your band measurement from your full bust measurement. Generally speaking, for each 1 inch (2.5 cm) in difference between the two measurements, the cup goes up by one size; so 1 inch (2.5 cm) is an "A" cup, 2 inches (5 cm) is a "B" cup, 3 inches (7.5 cm) is a "C" cup, 4 inches (10 cm) is a "D" cup, and so on.

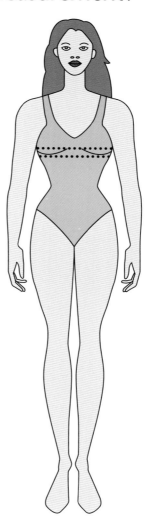

ABOVE The top line indicates the point where the bust is measured; the bottom line is the band measurement position.

Question 51:
How do I take a waist measurement?

The easiest way to take your waist measurement is to tie a piece of string around your waist until the fit is snug but comfortable. Now bend to each side of your body and then stand straight; the string should be sitting on your natural waistline. Use the tape measure to measure around the waist where the string is sitting, making sure not to hold your breath or pull the tape too tight.

Keep the string in place around the waist until you have finished taking all your body measurements as it's a useful marker for taking the back-neck to waist and other measurements.

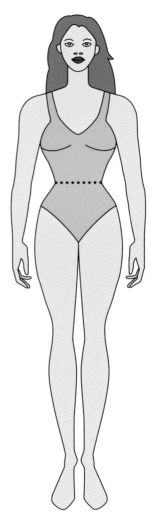

ABOVE It's important to measure your natural waistline, rather than where it may fall on any garments you wear.

Question 52:
How do I take a hip measurement?

To find your full hip measurement, stand with your legs and feet together and wrap the tape measure around the fullest area of your hips; this is usually 7–9 inches (18–23 cm) below the waistline. Keeping the string around your waist after taking the waist measurement (see Question 51) you will have no trouble finding the correct area.

For some people finding the full hip measurement may be misleading if choosing a pattern size from this measurement. If you have a large tummy and a small bottom, you may find it's beneficial to take the top hip measurement as well so you can compare the difference between top and full hip. The top hip is measured from 3 inches (7.5 cm) below the waist or from 4 inches (10 cm) above the full hip measurement. The top hip area is not marked on commercial patterns, but if you know you are not a standard size in this area, then it's worth taking the measurement and possibly adapting the pattern later.

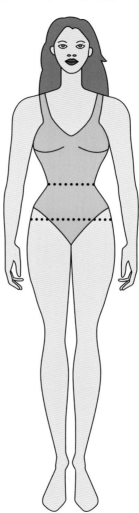

ABOVE The full hip measurement (bottom line) is 7–9 inches (18–23 cm) below the natural waistline.

Question 53:
How do I take a back-neck to waist measurement?

To take an accurate back-neck or nape to waist measurement you will definitely need a friend to help you. Stand with your back straight but relaxed, and arms down by your sides. Get your helper to find the most prominent backbone at the base of your neck and measure from that point to your natural waistline (still marked by the string from Question 51).

Compare your measurement to the back of the pattern envelope and the difference is how much you need to lengthen or shorten along the adjustment line marked on the front and back patterns.

EXPERT TIP

❝ The average back-neck to waist measurement for a U.S. size 12 is 16 inches (41 cm). This can go down to 15 inches (38 cm) for a short measurement, and up to 17½ inches (45 cm) for a long measurement. If you have a vastly different measurement from these guidelines, then try checking again. ❞

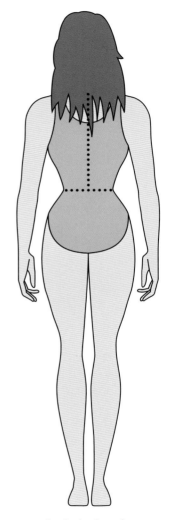

ABOVE Take the back-neck measurement from the nape of the neck to the natural waistline.

Question 54:
How do I take a sleeve measurement?

Measuring your sleeve length is not quite as straightforward as you think; it's easy to confuse the style of a sleeve—drop shoulders or raglan sleeves, for example—with the actual body measurement as there are different points to measure from. It's worth finding several different measurements that will be useful for all designs. You will need a friend to help, but once done you won't need to measure again as it's the one measurement that doesn't change with age.

Stand straight with your arm slightly bent and your hand lightly resting on your hip. Measure from the nape of the neck (the same point that you started the back-neck to waist measurement) and along the shoulder to the point where a set-in sleeve usually starts; this is the nape to shoulder measurement. Then measure from the same shoulder point down to the little bone that protrudes on your wrist; this is the shoulder to wrist measurement.

Other useful sleeve measurements are the top arm, measured at the fullest part just near the armpit, and the wrist measurement.

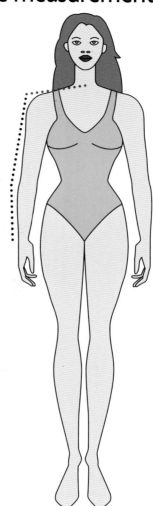

ABOVE Take two measurements for a sleeve; nape to shoulder (marked with a red line) and shoulder to wrist (the black line).

Question 55:
What other aspects of my body shape should I take into consideration?

Measurements are an essential part of determining your body shape so you can alter the pattern to fit you. But you should also consider any problem areas you have; you probably already know where you have difficulties on your body shape by being aware of any issues you have when buying clothes.

Study yourself; possibly your shoulders slope or you have one shoulder higher than the other—a very common problem. Or, when buying pants, do you find there's not enough room in the waist, but space in the hip and bottom area? Or does your back sway inward into the waist, making pants loose around the back waistband?

Be objective about your body shape and how your clothes fit. This enables you to identify fitting problems and develop skills in altering commercial patterns to fit.

Question 56:
What is "tolerance" or "ease"?

"Tolerance" or "ease" is the space left in a garment to allow you to move within it. Why does a garment sometimes fit perfectly and then another dress in the same size feel larger, even if the body measurements on the patterns are exactly the same? This is because there are two basic kinds of ease: wearing ease and design ease.

Wearing ease is the minimum amount of room added to your clothing to make it suitable for everyday activities, such as sitting and moving. It's the extra measurement added to your actual body measurements that allows for comfort. Generally, the accepted ease is 2½ inches (6.5 cm) around the bust, 1 inch (2.5 cm) at the waist, and 3 inches (7.5 cm) at the hip.

Design ease is generally considered to be beyond comfort ease. Depending on the design and personal preference, the amount of ease varies from a very fitted dress to a loose shirt, but it's incorporated into the design to create a certain silhouette or look.

Fabrics with plenty of stretch, such as jersey or lycra, that are made into dresses, sportswear, lingerie, and swimwear, require less ease in the pattern because the fabric has "built-in" ease.

Measurement position	Your measurement	Ease to add	Total measurement
Bust			
Waist			
Hip			
Front crotch length			
Back crotch length			
Wrist			

ABOVE Photocopy the above chart and fill it in with the relevant measurements when you need to work out the ease required for a pattern.

Question 57:
Can I adapt a tailor's dummy to my size?

There are three types of tailor's dummies: the display form, used for merchandising fashion in shop windows, which usually bears little resemblance to "normal" body measurements; the nonadjustable dummy generally used by the fashion industry and available in standard industry sizes; and the adjustable dummy, made for the domestic market, which can be adjusted at the bust, waist, and hip to achieve a custom shape.

All tailor's dummies are relatively expensive but if you are serious about making clothes, it's worth acquiring one. You may be able to find one secondhand. And don't worry if it's a nonadjustable dummy that's too small; you can pad it out to your shape.

Put a bra in your size onto the stand and stuff the cups with wadding.Pad out the waist and hips with batting or bandages to the desired size. Keep measuring to check the measurements match yours. When you have finished, cover the waist and hip area with jersey and attach with pins or, if possible, long stitches to create a firm base to pin on and measure when using.

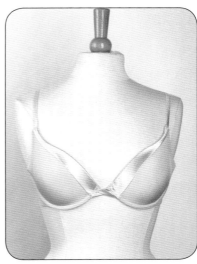

ABOVE Adapt a too-small dress form by dressing it in your own bra and then padding this out to the correct shape.

EXPERT TIP

❝ If you would like to have a dress form of your own body, www.threadsmagazine.com has a tutorial on how to make a duct-tape body mold. ❞

Question 58:
Is it worth making a "toile" or tester garment?

A "toile," also known as a "tester" or "pretest" garment, is a very rough first version of the garment you want to make. It's made quickly and without any refinements, but it enables you to see what the pattern's style and fit is like. It is not necessary to make a toile every time you make a new style but if you are unsure about the shape and fit, it's definitely worth it.

There are several reasons for making a toile. You might be making a semifitted or fitted item of clothing and want to achieve a great fit, which can be impossible if you haven't made the pattern before. Or, you may have bought fabric that is expensive or irreplaceable, and are feeling nervous about cutting it up and risking "ruining" it. Perhaps you have made a lot of alterations to the pattern and want to check that they are correct. Or maybe you are about to embark on a significant project such as a wedding dress or coat that you want to get just right before you begin.

A toile or tester garment means you can go ahead and produce a garment that you will feel proud and happy to wear. It might take an extra hour or two to make but it is certainly worth the effort.

Question 59:
What fabric should I use to make the toile?

Any cheap fabric will do for making a toile and for most projects, such as shirts, jackets, and shift-style dresses and skirts; a material called calico is useful. Available in different weights, calico is cheap and ideal for making toiles or testers. It's easy to find in most fabric shops as well as online. It's more cost effective to buy calico in quantity, which is usually anything over about 33 feet (10 m). Of course, if you have a supply of calico at home, you will find you are more likely to make a toile than if a special trip to the store is necessary.

If you are about to make a bias-cut dress with a cowl neckline, or a wraparound dress, then making the toile out of calico will not work, as the fabric doesn't mold or cling to the body. You need to choose a cheap fabric that emulates the "real" material. It's fairly easy to find cheap synthetic jersey or crepe if you want a fabric with drape.

ABOVE Calico is a plain-woven cotton fabric that doesn't fray easily. Pick a weight of calico that most closely matches the weight of your chosen final fabric.

Question 60:
How do I make the toile?

To make a toile, speed is of the essence; the faster you can do it, the quicker you can see the result. So first press the calico to get rid of any creases and fold the length in half, selvedge to selvedge. Lay out the pattern pieces on the cloth. Follow the layout plan on the instruction sheet, even if you find that the calico is a different width to your actual fabric. Cut out the pieces. It's not really necessary to cut out facings, top collars, and pockets unless you feel you want to make up the whole garment; the point of a toile is to quickly get a feel of the shape and fit.

Turn up the hems and press so that the toile shows the finished garment length. Mark any features like pockets, buttonhole positions, and center front or fold line onto the calico pieces with a pen or pencil. This is useful information for when you try on the toile.

Sew your toile together using exactly the same seam allowances that are marked on the pattern. Make sure you sew all darts and seams correctly; the more accurate you are, the better the fit. When sewing together a jacket or a top, do sew in both sleeves; it will distort the fit if you try on a half-finished garment. Press all seams open but don't bother with finishing the raw edges.

Question 61:
When I try on the toile, how do I know if it's a good fit?

Try on the toile, pinning the opening together, and stand back and have a look in the mirror. Don't be put off as calico—the fabric generally used to make a toile—is remarkably unflattering. If you like it now, you will love it in your "real" fabric!

First check how comfortable the garment is: Have you enough ease around the bust, waist, and hips?; Does it feel tight across the back?; Can you move your arms freely? Is the garment sitting well on the body with no wrinkles in places that could be a fitting problem; for example, creases around the waistline or back neck.

Look at the shoulders and, if it isn't a drop-shouldered style, check to see that they are not too wide. If you are making a jacket, insert different-size shoulder pads to see how each alters the shape.

When looking in the mirror and checking the fit of a toile, there is a temptation to overfit. However, this can be unflattering if you have a few bulges which are better left unseen.

If, having fitted the style to the best of your ability, you still feel indifferent about the design, this is the time to abandon the pattern, before you have wasted fabric and precious time. Don't feel downhearted but remember this is part of the process; in the fashion industry, two or three toiles might need to be made before a satisfactory garment is produced.

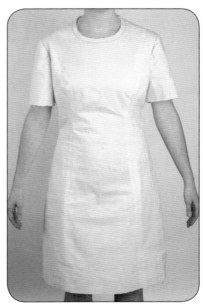

ABOVE A toile may not be the most flattering of garments but it will allow you to get an idea of what the finished project should look like.

Question 62:
Before I start, is there a sequence for pattern alterations?

When you adapt a pattern to your measurements, you often end up having to alter several parts of the pattern, so by the time you have finished this could be anywhere between five and ten different parts of the pattern. There isn't one definitive formula of how you should approach pattern alterations, but it is more important that you remember what you have done to each pattern piece and don't muddle up your different pieces as you go along.

The first area to take a look at is the back-neck to waist length. If this is an area you need to lengthen or shorten, alter the pattern at the waistline, and remember to change both the back and front parts of the pattern (and side front and side back, if applicable). It is important to alter the nape to waist first as it affects the total length of the garment. If you are making pants, lengthen or shorten the crotch length first.

The second area to be measured and adapted is the general length of the garment on the main bodice pieces, pant legs, skirt, and sleeves.

Now that you have the correct back-neck to waist and length, the fit of the style can be adjusted by making alterations to the bust, waist, and hip areas, as well as any design changes to necklines and collars.

Question 63:
How do I know what seam allowances there are?

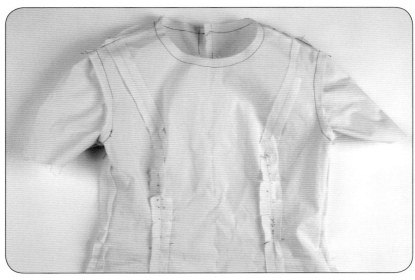

ABOVE Don't forget to sew accurate seam allowances when making up the toile, as this will have a bearing on the final fit.

Most commercial patterns have seam allowances of ⅝ inch (1.5 cm) everywhere, but it's definitely worth checking the information sheet before starting to sew. The circles on the pattern pieces also indicate the seam allowances. Some Burda patterns have no seam allowance, which can be easier and less confusing when altering the pattern. However, you have to remember to add your own seam allowances when cutting out these patterns.

In the fashion industry, seam allowances are generally smaller, with ⅜ inch (1 cm) being normal; side seams and center-back seams, however, are sometimes ⅝ inch (1.5 cm). This is mainly to save fabric but also it's faster and more accurate to put in a sleeve or a collar with a ⅜ inch (1 cm) allowance.

Question 64:
How do I measure the pattern?

It's worth taking time to measure the pattern before you cut your fabric and start making the garment, as it takes the risk out of knowing whether the finished style is going to fit.

Measuring the flat pattern determines the amount of ease it has in key areas such as the bust, waist, and hips. It tells you how much room a finished garment will have above and beyond your body measurements (see Question 56). This is vital if you know you have full hips or a large bust, for example, and need to compensate.

When measuring the pattern, it isn't necessary to cut out the pattern pieces exactly but it helps. Make sure you have all the pieces you need on hand before you begin.

To measure the hip area, place your ruler perpendicular to the grain line and across the widest area of the skirt pattern on the front and back pieces. Measure from seam to seam excluding allowances and space for pleats, tucks, or darts. Make sure you add front and back measurements together. Compare these measurements with yours; the difference is the amount of tolerance or ease the pattern has.

> ## EXPERT TIP
> ❝ When taking flat pattern measurements, use a highlighter to mark the measuring line from seam to seam on each pattern piece, perpendicular to the grain line. This will make it easier to see if you need to remeasure. ❞

The same principle is applied to the bust. When measuring the bust, find the fullest area on the pattern front and measure from the center front or fold line, excluding any seam allowances, to the side seam, running through the middle of the bust dart. Double to get the front measurement. On the pattern back, measure from the side seam under the armhole to the center back, excluding darts and seam allowances. Double this. Add the front and back together to get the bust measurement and deduct yours to get the ease.

You can refine a pattern's fit by adding or subtracting to the ease to suit your needs and figure shape.

65 Should I cut out each pattern piece provided?

66 Are there any techniques used when preparing pattern pieces?

67 How do I prolong the life of a tissue paper pattern?

68 Are there any tips before I start altering commercial patterns?

69 How can I tell the right side and wrong side of the fabric?

70 What is the grain of a fabric?

71 What does the bias mean?

72 What is the nap?

73 Is it necessary to preshrink fabric?

74 How do I straighten fabric before I begin?

75 How do I lay out the pattern on the fabric?

76 Is it necessary to pin the pattern to the fabric?

77 How do I make sure that the pattern is positioned on the fabric grain?

78 What is cutting "on the fold"?

79 Are there any shortcuts to cutting out the pattern on fabric?

80 How do I mark the darts and notches?

81 How do I mark other features?

82 How do I cut a pattern out of striped fabric?

83 How do I cut a pattern out of checked or plaid material?

84 How do I cut a pattern out of a printed fabric?

85 How do I cut out a fabric like velvet that has a nap?

86 How do I work with a slippery fabric such as chiffon or satin?

87 How do I cut a pattern out of a jersey or stretch material?

4

PREPARING THE PATTERN AND FABRIC

Question 65:
Should I cut out each pattern piece provided?

When you take out the pattern from the envelope, find each pattern piece you need by matching the letter and number with the chosen style (see Question 40). Usually there are patterns for several different styles included in the envelope, so the easiest method is to work out which pieces you need and then put all the other unwanted pattern pieces back into the envelope. Having found the relevant pattern pieces for your style, cut them out roughly, leaving a short margin around each piece.

Mark the size you are going to cut out; this can be confusing so its advisable to highlight the pattern (see Question 41). After checking that you have the correct size, cut out your pattern with paper scissors as accurately as you can just outside of the cutting line.

EXPERT TIP

66 If you slip and make a cut or tear in the tissue paper where you shouldn't have, simply fix it back into place as best you can with masking tape or cellophane tape. The important thing is that the shape is retained and that you can still read the markings. 99

Question 66:
Are there any techniques used when preparing pattern pieces?

Before cutting out the pattern in your size it's important to iron the pattern pieces to get rid of any folds or creases. Use the iron on medium heat without any steam and gently hold one end of the pattern piece while trying to avoid any "curling" of the tissue paper.

Another technique in preparing the pattern is to cut out any triangle or double-triangle notches on the edges of the pattern, so that they stick out from the edge. This makes them easier to see later and acts as a reminder to ensure you transfer the information to the fabric.

Question 67:
How do I prolong the life of a tissue paper pattern?

Commercial patterns are lightweight and small and include multiple styles in one envelope, but the tissue paper on which they are printed is flimsy and tears easily.

Once you have found a pattern that you like, you may want to keep it and make it up again in a different fabric or perhaps use the pattern pieces for another project. This is when you will find it's worth spending a little time on prolonging the life of the tissue paper.

Cut out pieces of interfacing in the shape of the pattern pieces and fuse with the glue side up to the reverse side of the pattern pieces. Start with the iron in the middle of the pattern piece and work your way to the edges of the pattern.

You can use up scraps of interfacing left over from other projects as you don't have to be exact and overlapping pieces of interfacing won't matter.

The pattern pieces can be rolled and stored in cardboard tubes.

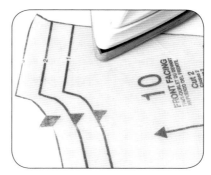

ABOVE Iron pattern pieces onto fusible interfacing to make them last longer.

Question 68:
Are there any tips before I start altering commercial patterns?

The excitement of wanting to get on with making a garment often means that the time spent altering a pattern is rushed. However, the more time you spend on perfecting the pattern, the better the final fit.

Start by preparing a clean, flat spacious work surface with only the required pattern pieces, your body measurements, and measuring equipment on hand. Being methodical and working through the pattern in a step-by-step way eliminates any chance of overlooking something. For example, if you alter the hip area on the front panel, remember to do the same on the back panel.

When it's necessary to add or subtract large amounts from an area—anything over 1 inch

(2.5 cm)—divide the amount between two or three different places. For example, if you are increasing the bust area on a panelled dress, divide the amount you need to add on between the front, side front, side back, and back pattern pieces. Remember there is a pair for each pattern piece and any amount added to one piece will be doubled in the fabric cut out.

As most commercial patterns have seam allowances included, it can be confusing when comparing the pattern's measurements to your own body measurements. Mark the seam allowance (see Question 63) in red felt tip on the pattern pieces to give you the net amount without the seam allowances.

Question 69:
How can I tell the right side and wrong side of the fabric?

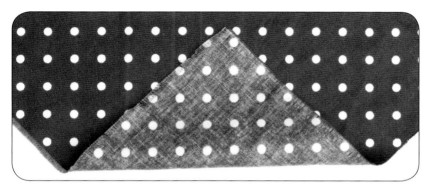

ABOVE On a printed fabric, the color and pattern is stronger on the right side.

Sometimes finding the right side of fabric can be tricky as many fabrics have virtually identical right and wrong sides. The right side of the fabric is the side that shows on the garment and the wrong side is inside, next to the body. If the two sides are the same, decide on which side is to be your right side and then be consistent and cut all pattern pieces the same. Once you have chosen your right side, mark it with tailor's chalk near the selvedge to help as a reminder.

If the right side of a fabric is not obvious, there are a few ways you can tell. For example, look at how the fabric is folded when it's purchased; cottons and linens are folded with the right side out, and woollens with the wrong side out. It's fairly easy to spot the right side on prints, as the color is usually clearer and brighter on that side.

If you have ever examined the selvedge on a length of fabric, you may have noticed two rows of little holes. This is where the fabric has been placed on a frame during the manufacturing process. The fabric is placed on the frame, right side up, onto pin bars that punch little holes along the selvedge. The "rough" side of the selvedge—where the holes are pushed through—is normally the right side of the fabric.

Question 70:
What is the grain of a fabric?

The grain or grain line refers to the direction of the yarns in woven fabric. It has an important effect on the way the garment hangs and drapes. There are three types of grain lines to consider.

The first is the warp or lengthwise grain, formed by the threads that run the length of the fabric, parallel to the selvedge. Second is the weft or crosswise grain, formed by the threads that run perpendicular to the selvedge and the cut edge of the fabric as it comes off the roll.

The third grain line is the bias grain. This refers to any line that falls at a diagonal angle to the selvedge, but the true bias falls at a 45-degree angle (see Question 71).

The warp yarns are tightly stretched during the weaving process and so the lengthwise grain has very little or no stretch. Warp yarns are durable, hold their shape well, and resist bagging and stretching. Most garments, therefore, are cut so the lengthwise grain runs vertically, perpendicular to the hem.

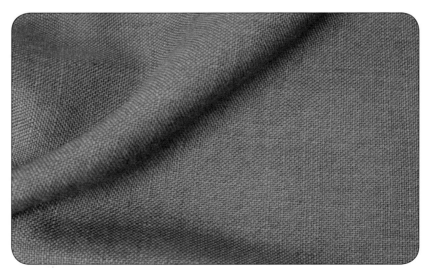

ABOVE In some fabrics, the direction of the warp and weft grains is very obvious.

Question 71:
What does the bias mean?

ABOVE If you pull a fabric across the bias, you will see how much it stretches.

The term "bias" is used to describe the grain line that lies at a 45-degree angle to the lengthwise and crosswise grain of the fabric.

In woven fabrics the bias grain produces a stretch. This stretch is much more than you get from either the lengthwise or crosswise grain. Cutting fabric on the bias is very different from cutting material on the straight grain.

Garments cut on the bias softly accentuate body lines as well as curves. Cutting a full skirt in a satin on the bias would achieve a soft drape over the hips and hang in folds below the knees.

Making a garment cut on the bias can be very rewarding but choose a simple style if you want to use a bias cut. Elaborate seams and complicated construction details—such as inserting zippers—can be a headache. Always hang a bias-cut garment for at least twenty-four hours before hemming it, as it tends to drop.

Question 72:
What is the nap?

ABOVE When you "scrunch" up a piece of velvet so the fabric is arranged in different directions, the pile and the effect of the nap becomes obvious.

A fabric with a nap usually has a "pile"; velvet, corduroy, and suede all have a nap. Such fabrics are not smooth, but have a fuzzy, furlike surface. If you stroke a napped fabric and sweep the pile in a different direction it can appear to change shade, depending which way you stroked it.

On the back of a pattern envelope you will see different quantities and layouts given for fabrics with and without nap. Generally, the nap runs upward on garments. More importantly, when you lay out your pattern pieces the nap should run in the same direction on each piece.

If you are in doubt about the direction of the nap, there are several ways to check it. Try brushing the fabric with your hand one way and then brush the area next to that spot in the other direction. Check to see if the fabric looks the same when brushed in both directions. Another way of confirming the direction of the nap is to use a length of fabric and fold it lengthwise and lay the two directions next to each other, then examine the fabric to see if it looks the same from each direction.

Question 73:
Is it necessary to preshrink fabric?

When you buy your fabric, hopefully the store will supply laundering instructions. If not, remember to ask for them before you leave, as it really is important to know how to care for the fabric, both before and after garment construction. It's surprising how many fabrics you might think are machine washable turn out not to be; some linens, for example, are dry-clean only.

It's not necessary to preshrink every piece of fabric before you cut out the pattern but be aware that with certain materials, such as cheap cotton, it's a wise precaution.

Wool does need to be preshrunk before cutting out, but don't put it in your washer and dryer, or you will end up with a piece of felt!

HOW IT'S DONE

• Place the woollen fabric on your ironing board.
• Set your iron to the wool setting and select steam.
• Carefully steam along the entire length. In some cases you will actually see the material shrinking.
• This method can also be used for densely woven "tapestry-style" fabrics.

Question 74:
How do I straighten fabric before I begin?

When you buy fabric you will often find when you come to fold it and lay out your pattern that the fabric was cut at an angle in the store; this can make it difficult to see the grain line. It might be necessary to straighten the ends; this can be done easily on woven cloth using one of two methods.

One method is to make a small nip or cut in the selvedge of the fabric near the end of the length. Tease out one thread on the edge of this cut and pull it gently, across the width of the fabric. As you pull it out, the fabric will pucker, but once

the thread has gone, a gap will be left in the fabric. This gap is running along the crosswise grain line. Trim the end of the fabric to this gap. Fold the fabric in half lengthwise, matching the selvedges and newly cut grain edge and pin the edges together. Now smooth the fold line; if it lies flat you have succeeded.

An easier way is to make a snip through the selvedge and simply tear across the width of the fabric. You should have a straight end, which may need pressing. This works well on lining fabric but not jersey or some woven fabrics.

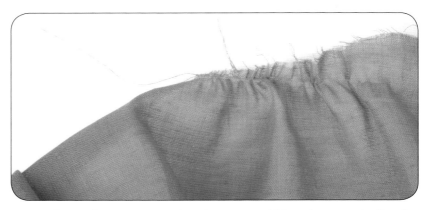

ABOVE If you pull out a crosswise thread on a piece of fabric, the material will pucker as you go. However, it will lie straight again once you've pulled the thread out.

Question 75:
How do I lay out the pattern on the fabric?

The instruction sheet inside the pattern envelope will give you suggested layout diagrams for various fabric widths. When you have found the best layout for your pattern and fabric width, check that the pattern pieces fit onto your fabric before you begin cutting.

With the fabric folded, selvedge to selvedge and right sides together, try and lay out the entire amount of the fabric you are going to use on a table. Try not to have part of the length hanging off the edge of the table while pinning and cutting, as the extra weight at the end can cause distortion and stretching. If the fabric doesn't fit onto the table, fold or roll up the end that's not being cut and carefully unroll as your layout progresses.

ABOVE Make sure you have everything on hand before beginning to lay out a pattern, and make sure all the pieces fit on the fabric before cutting.

Question 76:
Is it necessary to pin the pattern to the fabric?

Having laid out the pattern on the fabric the main aim is to keep the pattern on the grain line and to be able to cut out the pattern accurately. This means pinning the tissue paper pattern to the fabric to stop it from moving. As you place your pins into the pattern and fabric, keep your fabric as flat as possible on the cutting surface. As tempting as it may be, don't lift the fabric and put your hand underneath to pin as this could alter the position of the pattern on the fabric.

As you pin, position your pattern pieces on the grain line (see Question 77), keeping the pieces close together so there is no fabric wastage. Smooth the tissue flat as you go. Place pins 2–3 inches (5–7.5 cm) apart into your pattern and fabric, close to the edges of the pattern pieces. On large pieces dot a few pins around the center of the pattern. Don't cover the pattern and fabric with too many pins as this will bunch up the tissue paper and distort the pattern.

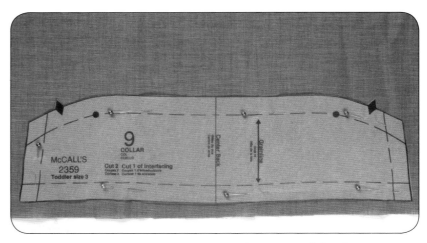

ABOVE Place pins 2–3 inches (5–7.5 cm) apart and running parallel to the pattern edge. Avoid using too many pins, especially on smaller pattern pieces.

Question 77:
How do I make sure that the pattern is positioned on the fabric grain?

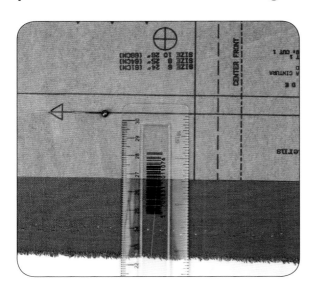

LEFT Measure from the grain line marked on the pattern down to the selvedge.

Every commercial pattern piece marks the recommended grain line so that the garment will fit according to the designer's intentions. The pattern marking that indicates the lengthwise grain (see Question 44) should be positioned parallel to the fabric selvedge. Pin one end of the grain line to the fabric, then measure down to the selvedge. Position the other end of the grain line the same measurement from the selvedge and pin in place. Even small pieces

such as cuffs and facings work best if you follow the grain line, and especially collars, which have a tendency to twist if not cut on the true grain. If you want to experiment with different fabrics and try making a bias-cut garment, mark a new straight grain line on the pattern piece at a 45-degree angle to the printed arrow. This would increase the drape and make interesting use of stripes and other fabric designs. Plan carefully before you cut out diagonal stripes as it can be confusing.

Question 78:
What is cutting "on the fold"?

On your instruction sheet the layout plans may indicate placing the edges of some pattern pieces directly on the fold line of your fabric, often the front of a dress or skirt. This is to make it easier to cut out both the right and left sides of a much larger piece as one.

Straighten your fabric (see Question 74) and fold in half lengthways, selvedge to selvedge, smoothing out any wrinkles as you go. If you fold the fabric right sides together, this speeds up the preparation of pieces for stitching, as often you need to sew pattern parts with right sides together. However, if you are cutting out a plaid or print fabric, folding the fabric wrong sides together makes matching checks and positioning of a floral print easier.

To lay your pattern piece on the fold line, put the solid edge of the pattern right against the fold of your fabric. When you cut out the piece remember not to cut along the folded edge!

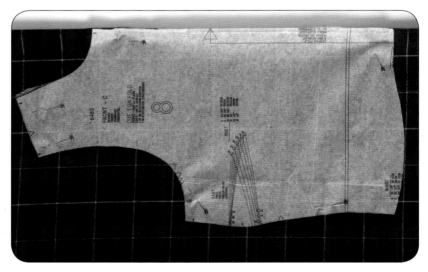

ABOVE If a pattern piece needs to be pinned along the folded edge of the fabric, this is clearly marked along the relevant edge of the pattern.

Question 79:
Are there any shortcuts to cutting out the pattern on fabric?

Accuracy is crucial when cutting out your pattern, and laying out your pattern on the fabric with the correct grain line is fundamental for a successful garment. The other important stage is to transfer the construction symbols and notches to the fabric; this is the final step before you start sewing.

If you have ironed the pattern pieces flat, when you place them on the fabric you can speed up the process slightly by using weights (heavy stones work well) to hold the pattern down. This keeps the pattern pieces in place while you pin them down.

Instead of cutting around the notches by making tricky protruding triangles, carefully nip into the seam allowance at the notches. This cuts down on time you spend marking up the fabric pieces.

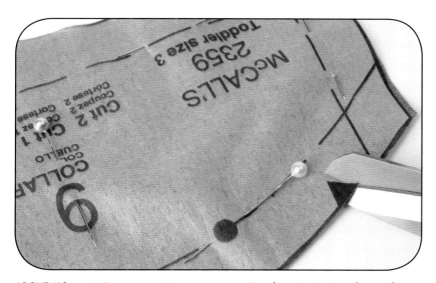

ABOVE When cutting out a pattern you can save time by snipping into the notches to mark their position on the fabric.

Question 80:
How do I mark the darts and notches?

Depending on your fabric, there are several different ways to mark darts and notches. You may want to use tailor's tacks, tailor's chalk, or fade-away pens. If you use markers, test them on a scrap of your fabric first to check that they are removable. Mark on the wrong side of the fabric or in the seam allowance of the right side.

The amount of information transferred depends on how much experience you have. A beginner may need to mark every pleat and gather. However, the more experienced may need to mark only the notches, darts, and pockets.

Tailor's chalk is a very useful and quick way of marking darts. Find the point on the pattern and mark with a pin, then lift the tissue paper and chalk the position of the

end of the pin on the fabric.

Another way to mark darts is by using a pattern wheel and dressmaker's carbon. Fold your fabric piece (with pattern still attached) at the dart, with the wrong sides together. Fold a piece of the carbon paper in half and insert it between the two layers of fabric. Trace over the dart line with the tracing wheel and you will see the color on the fabric clearly marking the stitching line.

Notches (see Question 42) are triangular symbols used all around the pattern to match pieces together. You can mark them by cutting them out on the fabric edge, so triangles of fabric protrude; by drawing them on with a marker; or by snipping them out of the allowance (see Question 79).

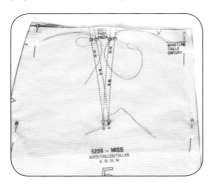

LEFT One way to mark darts is to use tailor's tacks; basting stitches taken through the pattern and fabric, which are snipped and then left in place when the pattern is unpinned from the fabric.

Question 81:
How do I mark other features?

Other design features on a pattern may be pockets and zipper placements. It's important to mark pockets correctly on the front pattern pieces when they are flat and lined up next to each other, to make sure you don't end up with one pocket higher than the other.

Basting or tacking in a contrasting color is a fairly quick way of marking a pocket. It's more durable than using tailor's tacks, which have a habit of disappearing while the garment is being made up. Alternatively, mark the position with tailor's chalk.

HOW IT'S DONE

There's an easy way to accurately mark the position of a symbol with tailor's chalk.
• Push a pin through the pattern at the symbol—for example, one of the dots— and then through the fabric.
• Where the pin comes out, rub the fabric with the tailor's chalk.

Question 82:
How do I cut a pattern out of striped fabric?

Making a garment out of a striped fabric can be a great way to add an individual look to the style of a garment, whether you choose to use the stripes crosswise, lengthwise, or diagonally.

To work out if your stripe is even or not, fold the fabric lengthwise (if you can only see the stripes on the right side of the fabric, fold the material right side to right side) and then turn back one corner to form a 45-degree diagonal. If the stripes are even, they will match along the angle in width, color, and sequence. Uneven stripes will have variations and will not match.

When deciding which direction to lay out the pattern pieces on the fabric, think about how the stripes will meet at the seams and darts. Always remember to allow for seam allowances when matching stripes. If you decide to use the stripe diagonally or on the bias, the stripes will form chevrons down the seam, which needs careful planning to ensure they match before cutting. Unless you have an even stripe, it's easier to cut in single layers.

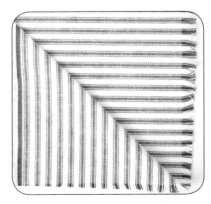

ABOVE If your stripes are evenly spaced, they should match up when the fabric is folded back in this manner.

Question 83:
How do I cut a pattern out of checked or plaid material?

Cutting out and making a garment in check or plaid material always needs extra time since you have to plan carefully where the checks should end up on the finished garment. Do you want the most prominent lines in the check to run on the bias (diagonally), or horizontally, or vertically? The important thing to remember with checks or plaids, is not to cut until you are sure everything is in the correct position.

When buying checked or plaid material you should purchase some extra fabric to allow for matching the pattern, and for the odd mistake. Look on the pattern envelope for where it guides you on how to calculate fabric usage with napped fabric, and use this to estimate the amount to buy.

There is a vast range of checked and plaid fabrics available, with patterns in different sizes and colors (see Question 19). Some checks and plaids appear to have irregular squares and bars, while others have a symmetrical look. To check whether your pattern is even and regular, fold it as for striped fabric—see Question 82.

When cutting out plaid fabrics it's impossible to match every area, so you need to give priority to those parts of the garment that are most visible. The middle of the check usually runs vertically through the center front, center back, and down the center of the sleeve. The check runs horizontally across the chest area.

Question 84:
How do I cut a pattern out of a printed fabric?

Before laying your sewing pattern onto any fabric that features a pattern, you need to check what sort of pattern is on the fabric. Is there a distinctive top and bottom to the design or does it seem to run both ways through the fabric?

A one-way print has a distinct top and bottom to the design; for example, on a design that features animals their feet will be at the bottom and their heads will be at the top. With this type of print it's necessary to lay all the pattern pieces in one direction to make sure you don't have one animal upside down! You are likely to need more fabric to cut a directional or one-way print so follow the "nap" fabric quantities on the pattern envelope. With a pronounced print you will want to match certain areas, but matching every seam is impossible, so stick to areas that catch the eye, such as side seams and center back.

With a two-way print, it's easier to lay and cut out the pattern, as you are not restricted by the direction. You can use either end for the top of the garment.

Question 85:
How do I cut out a fabric like velvet that has a nap?

Cutting out velvet is not difficult once you know what to do. However, one thing to remember is that velvet is not as forgiving as other fabrics and you need to take some care when pinning, cutting, and constructing.

Before laying out a pattern on velvet, you need to establish the direction of the nap, as this determines how the garment will look when it's finished. If the nap runs up, the fabric feels rough and the color is richer and darker; this is the preferred way for velvet. If the nap runs down, the fabric feels smooth and the color is lighter and shinier.

When pinning the pattern pieces onto the velvet, it's better to use fewer pins than usual, since the velvet seems to bunch the tissue paper up, making it harder to be accurate when cutting. You may find it simpler to cut velvet, especially silk or viscose velvet, as a single layer rather than double, as there will be less slippage. If cutting a single layer, remember to reverse the pattern if you need a pair.

There are a few tips when working with velvet that can reduce the frustration. Always use a steam iron and press right-side down on

EXPERT TIP

❝ Drape the uncut velvet over yourself and look in the mirror, the pile should be running upwards and look rich and dark. Run your hand over the nap to check its direction. Use tailor's chalk near the selvedge and mark the correct direction with an arrow. ❞

top of an old towel; this helps to keep the pile from getting squashed. Never iron the right side, or let the full weight of the iron rest on the fabric; only use the point of the iron to press seams open.

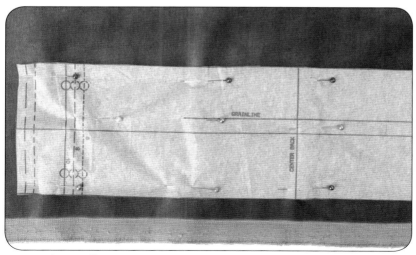

ABOVE It's generally easier to pin your pattern pieces onto a single layer of velvet. Use only a few pins and smooth the pattern out as you pin.

Question 86:
How do I work with a slippery fabric such as chiffon or satin?

Cutting out slippery fabric can be a headache but it is worth a little preparation time to reduce the pain.

Before laying out the fabric on the cutting surface, place a sheet of paper under the fabric first. You can use dot-and-cross paper (see Question 6) but if you don't have any, use a lightweight paper; tissue paper will do. With lightweight and slippery fabric the grain line distorts easily, so check if it's accurate, then

EXPERT TIP

❝ If you are cutting out a slippery fabric that is machine washable, spray with spray starch when you lay out the fabric. Cutting out will be easier as well as constructing. Wash when you have finished making the garment. ❞

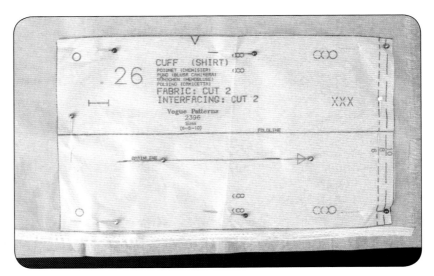

ABOVE Place a sheet of tissue paper on your cutting surface and then lie the fabric on top. Put the pattern piece on the fabric and then pin through all the layers.

pin the fabric to the paper around the edges. Lay the pattern on the fabric and pin through all layers. Cut out with either a rotary cutter or a sharp pair of scissors and cut using long even strokes rather than short choppy ones, as this helps produce a smooth line rather than jagged edges. Cutting silk rapidly makes your scissors become blunt and you may find you need to sharpen them more regularly.

Question 87:
How do I cut a pattern out of a jersey or stretch material?

Jersey or stretch fabric requires careful handling when cutting the pattern. Knits or jerseys are constructed differently than woven fabrics as they are made up of rows of interlocking loops. These fabrics often have no selvedges so therefore have no obvious grain line.

If you are struggling to fold your fabric, start by folding it in half and lining up the lengthwise edges. Try to keep the knit stitches parallel and then pin the fabric together.

Steam iron very gently, but don't press the iron onto the fabric.

Place your pattern pieces onto to the fabric and be careful not to stretch the jersey. As you pin the pattern pieces onto the fabric, make sure that both lie flat, since it's easy to distort the fabric as you pin. It may take a few tries, as stretch fabric can be slippery and difficult to work with. You may find a rotary cutter and self-seal mat useful when cutting out jersey.

88 How do I know if the bust darts are the right size?

89 My bustline is higher than that on the pattern; how do I raise the darts?

90 How do I lower bust darts?

91 I have a large bust; how do I alter a pattern with darts?

92 How do I alter the pattern for a small bust?

93 How do I make the bust area bigger on a princess seam bodice?

94 How do I take in a princess seam at the bust?

95 The pattern is tight over my back but fine over my bust; how do I alter?

96 The bodice is loose across my back; can I change this?

97 My shoulders are narrow; how do I shorten the length of the shoulder seam?

98 I have broad shoulders; how do I lengthen the measurement of the shoulder seam?

99 When I have made alterations to a pattern, how do I get the lines and angles to meet?

100 One shoulder is higher than the other; how can I compensate for this?

101 How do I change the shape of a neckline?

102 The front of the neckline is gaping; how can I fix this?

103 The back neck is gaping; how do I alter the pattern?

104 The front of the neckline is too loose; how do I decrease here?

105 The neck is too tight; how can I increase it?

106 How do I add gathers to a neckline?

107 How do I alter a pattern if I have a large bust and large tummy but narrow waist?

108 The positions of the buttonholes on my pattern aren't right for me; what should I do?

5

ADJUSTING BODICES AND TOPS

Question 88:
How do I know if the bust darts are the right size?

For a garment to be both comfortable and attractive, it should fit correctly. It shouldn't be too large or too small and it should fit around the con tours of the body without sagging, straining, or wrinkling.

The look of a dress or top is greatly affected by the undergarments you are wearing. A bra that fits you properly is essential since it affects the way the fabric drapes over the bust area. A good-fitting bra smoothes out any bulges and eliminates lumps and bumps. If you wear a bra that is too small, it's impossible for the dress or top to fit well.

You will know if the fit is wrong around the bust area if there are visible wrinkles above or below your bust, or any fullness in the fabric. And if the fit is wrong, chances are the darts are the wrong size. The bust darts should point to the fullest part of the bust and end about 1 inch (2.5 cm) from the nipple.

Question 89:
My bustline is higher than that on the pattern; how do I raise the darts?

It's actually fairly unusual for your bustline to be higher than marked on the pattern. If it is, then maybe your bra is making your bust higher than it is naturally. It's worth changing your bra and remeasuring yourself to see if this has any effect. It is also possible that the bust dart on the pattern is in the wrong place.

The bust dart is the arrow shape that points in from the side seam under the arm toward the bust. You will also find bust darts that point up from the waist toward the bust.

There is a simple way to raise the dart position (which could also be used to lower the dart slightly). Lay out your front bodice pattern and, with a ruler and pencil, draw a line through the center of both side and bottom darts; extend the lines so that they meet. This point is the apex or bust point. Measure the pattern from the middle of the shoulder seamline to the apex and compare this measurement to your own, taken from the middle of your shoulder to the nipple. The difference between the two is how much the dart should be raised. Once you have found your new bust point or apex, mark it on the pattern and then draw a line between the new point and the center of both darts. Reposition the end of each dart on this line; draw in the new darts, maintaining their position at the side seam and waist.

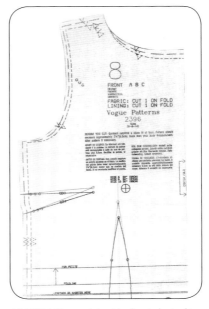

ABOVE When raising the bust dart, alter the position of the end of the dart; keep the dart in the same position at the side seam and waistline.

Question 90:
How do I lower bust darts?

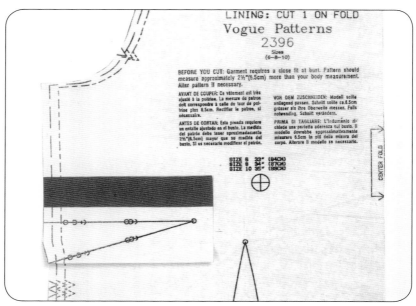

ABOVE To move a bust dart down, cut a flap out of the pattern around the dart and then fold into the new position. Fill the gap you have left with some paper.

If you need to lower bust darts by more than 1 inch (2.5 cm) you will need this method rather than redrawing the dart position as shown in Question 89. Lay out your bodice pattern and locate the dart running into the side seam. Draw a three-sided box around the existing dart so that it can be moved. Cut along the top and side lines you have drawn. Calculate how far down you want to move the dart and then fold the flap you have cut out of the pattern down toward the waist to move the position of the dart. Place paper underneath the gap you've made where the dart once was and stick it in place using masking tape; the paper will stablize the pattern where the gap has been cut. Check that the alterations are correct and redraw the side seam cutting line. Cut away excess paper to properly reshape the dart at the side seam.

Question 91:
I have a large bust; how do I alter a pattern with darts?

A large bust makes clothes appear to be shorter in the front than the back. You may also have noticed a wrinkle or fold of fabric starting at the armhole heading toward the bust, a sign that the bust area is not full enough. It's also worth bearing in mind that commercial patterns are designed to fit a "B" cup bra size.

One method of increasing the bust area by small amounts is to add at the side seams as well as adding the same amount to the sleeve. However, if you have a large bust, the fit won't be perfect with the side seam method as you need more room in the actual bust area, not the general circumference of the garment.

Lay out your front bodice pattern and draw a line from the middle of the shoulder through to the bust point or apex (see Question 89) then a line to the waist. Draw three evenly spaced lines from the armhole seam to the line running from shoulder to bust point. Cut along the line from waist to bust point and from bust point to shoulder. Cut along the lines that run from the armhole seam. Now spread the pattern apart at the bust point until you have added the extra room you need. Adjust the sections you have cut at the armhole as necessary to keep the shape at the armhole. Slip a sheet of paper under your adjusted pattern and then tape everything together. Check that the new armhole fits the sleeve in case of any distortion.

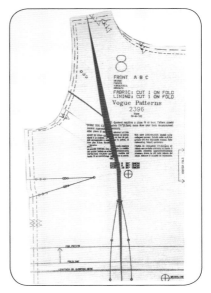

ABOVE To add room for a large bust, you need to increase the bodice front without altering the sleeve seam.

Question 92:
How do I alter the pattern for a small bust?

If you have a small bust you may find that the dart is creating too much fullness and there is extra fabric over the bust.

One way to reduce the bust area is to increase the size of the dart, but this will only work for small amounts of ¾ inch (2 cm) or less. If you take out too much, you will find the finished dart pokes out at the tapered end.

To decrease the bust area significantly for a pattern with a dart the following method works

but you may need to make a quick toile to be sure. Lay out the front bodice pattern and draw a line from the side seam through the center of the dart to the bust point. Then draw a line from the bust point to the center front with the line perpendicular to the center front. Cut along the new lines. Overlap the pattern tissue by the amount you want to reduce the bust, then redraw the dart which is now narrower. When you're happy with the result tape the pieces together.

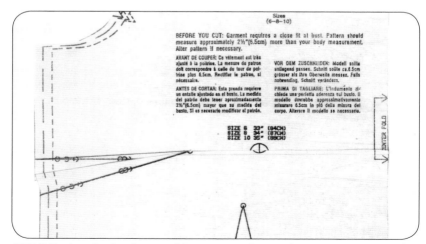

ABOVE To alter the dart for a small bust, you need to cut the pattern in two to make the adjustment. Tape the two pieces together when you've redrawn the dart.

Question 93:
How do I make the bust area bigger on a princess seam bodice?

Princess seams are a very good solution if you have a large bust, as they are easily altered to whatever size you need. Instead of having one pattern for the front of the garment, the front is split into two pieces, the front and side front. If you increase the size of the bust area, both pieces must be altered or you will find the seams won't match and the front will not sit correctly.

Lay out both pattern pieces. Start by drawing a horizontal line on the side front piece from under the armhole on the side seam through to the bust point (this is the fullest area of the curved edge). Draw a line across the front pattern piece in the same position.

Cut along the line on the side front, stopping within ¼ inch (5 mm) of the side seam—this acts as a "hinge" on your pattern. Place paper under the slashed pattern and spread apart at the bust by ⅝ inch (1.5 cm) for each cup size you want to increase, tapering to nothing at the hinged side seam. The grain line will have distorted slightly, but redraw it following the original line on the pattern. Tape the paper in place and

ABOVE On a pattern with princess seams you need to alter both the side front and front pattern pieces.

trim its edge to follow the curve of the original pattern at the bust.

To alter the front pattern piece, cut across the drawn line, place paper underneath, and then separate the two pieces by the same amount as the side front. Tape the pieces together. Remember to alter any facings and linings by the same amount and always check that the seams between the side front and front still match.

Question 94:
How do I take in a princess seam at the bust?

In a garment that is too big over a small bust the fabric will collapse over the bust area and the curve of the princess seams will be quite pronounced and may need refining.

If the problem is just too much curve on the bust, then you can redraw the side front to flatten out the curve without having to touch the front panel. Check that the side front and front seams match after altering.

To take out the bust fullness, first cut the side front and front pieces in the same way as described in Question 93. Then overlap the side front by the amount you want to decrease, tapering to nothing at the hinged side seam. Overlap the front piece by the same amount. Check that the seams between the pieces still match and then tape together. Redraw cutting lines and remember to alter facings and linings.

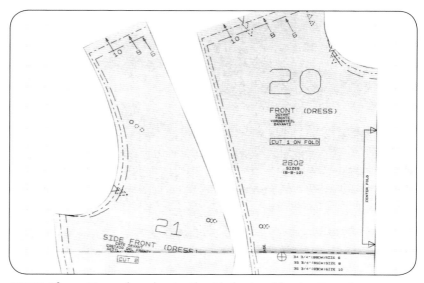

ABOVE After cutting and overlapping the side front and front pattern pieces, remember to redraw the grain line or any cutting lines.

Question 95:
The pattern is tight over my back but fine over my bust; how do I alter?

It's one of the most uncomfortable fitting problems when the front of a garment fits well but you are unable to drive or reach onto a shelf, as the back feels tight and the sleeves ride up your arms.

Lay out the back pattern piece and draw a line from the center of the shoulder to the bottom of the garment. Cut along the line, stopping within ¼ inch (5 mm) of the bottom to leave a "hinge". Place some paper under the pattern and then open up at the shoulder, tapering to nothing at the bottom of the garment. Generally speaking, to increase the back measurement by one size you need to add ⅝ inch (1.5 cm) with this amount being halved between the two back pattern pieces.

When you have finished the alteration you will see that the back shoulder seam is slightly longer than the front shoulder seam. However, you should be able to ease this extra into the front shoulder. If you have added a large amount and can't ease

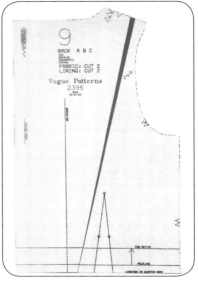

ABOVE To take the tightness out of the back of a garment, increase the pattern over the back of the shoulder.

the extra into the front shoulder, then you may need to add a small dart on the back shoulder roughly parallel with the armhole, the same width as the pattern alteration and about 3¼–4 inches (8–10 cm) long.

Question 96:
The bodice is loose across my back; can I change this?

If you have a very straight back and good posture you may find the fabric on a dress or jacket looks baggy and loose at the back; this suggests that you have a narrow back.

A good design for a narrow back is one with panels and style seams running from the shoulder to the hem. This makes it easy to take in where necessary.

If you have a back pattern piece with instructions to cut on the fold and want to alter for a narrow back, it is a good idea to make a seam down the center back where the "cut on fold" line is marked. You'll end up with two back pieces rather than one. By simply adding a seam allowance you can immediately shape the back to fit.

If you are working with a pattern that has two pieces for the back, then all you need to do is reduce the pattern at the back seam. Using a ruler, draw in a new cutting line

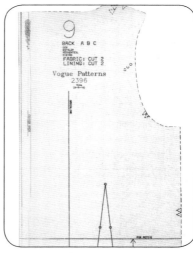

ABOVE To reduce the width across the back on a pattern you can draw in a new cutting line along the back seam.

along the back. Divide the amount you want to reduce the pattern by between the two pieces. Remember to alter the position of any fastenings, such as zippers, buttons, and buttonholes.

Question 97:
My shoulders are narrow; how do I shorten the length of the shoulder seam?

If your sleeves seem to hang over the edge of your shoulders and there are vertical wrinkles near the armhole opening, then you may have narrow shoulders.

Shoulder width is particularly important in fitted garments with set-in sleeves, but not as important in the overall fit of loose-fitting garments with drop shoulder seams or loose kimono sleeve styling.

Work out how much you need to alter the shoulder line; generally between ⅜–⅝ inch (1–1.5 cm). Lay out the front pattern and make a mark at the armhole the required amount below the shoulder seam. Draw a line from this point to the neck edge, tapering to nothing.

You also need to lower the bottom of the armhole by the same amount, or the armhole will be too tight. Mark the required amount on the side seam below the armhole. Using your curved ruler, redraw the armhole, tapering the line to the first set of notches. Repeat the process on the back pattern piece. When altered, check that the back and front shoulder seams and the side seams still match. Trim the

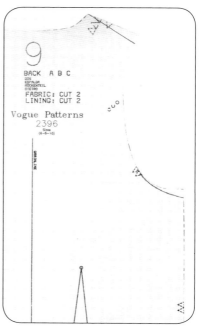

ABOVE If you lower the shoulder seam on a pattern, you also need to lower the bottom edge of the armhole. Remember to alter both front and back pieces.

pattern to the new cutting line. Since the size of the armhole does not change, this alteration should not affect the sleeve but you should check that the sleeve still fits in the adjusted armhole.

Question 98:
I have broad shoulders; how do I lengthen the measurement of the shoulder seam?

If you have broad shoulders, it's common to feel restricted in the armhole area and you may find that the sleeve sometimes rides up over the shoulder.

To lengthen at the shoulders, you need to do the reverse of Question 97. Lay out the front pattern piece and start by taping extra paper onto the existing pattern at the shoulder. Add your required amount at the armhole edge, tapering to nothing at the neck. Trim off any excess paper.

The armhole must also be altered; raise it by the same amount that you added to the shoulder under the armhole on the side seam. Tape on some extra paper at the armhole and draw in the new cutting line, starting the required amount above the side seam. Use a curved ruler to get the curve of the armhole correct. The same procedure is necessary on the back shoulder and armhole. When the alteration is done, check that the front and back side seams match and the armholes, when placed together, have a smooth curve.

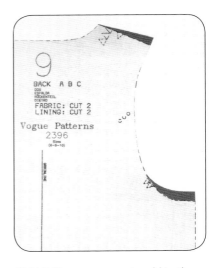

ABOVE Use extra paper to add to the pattern at the shoulder seam and the corresponding amount at the armhole.

Question 99:
When I have made alterations to a pattern, how do I get the lines and angles to meet?

Alterations are made to patterns either by cutting them apart and adding in new sections or paper, or by folding or overlapping parts of the pattern. The former will englarge a pattern; the latter will reduce it in size. After you've done these alterations, you are often left with a few discrepancies along the cutting lines. These won't line up as they did before and this can be confusing especially around armholes and necklines.

When altering for a full bust, for example (see Question 91), you may find that there is some distortion at the armhole and the reassembled pieces may no longer form a smooth curve. This is where your curved ruler comes in handy; use it to draw in a new armhole curve. Don't worry if you have to omit a little of the pattern in the process. There is no problem adding or subtracting from the pattern by tiny amounts; achieving a smooth line is more important. Remember that the human body is not made up of straight lines and no angles!

Question 100:
One shoulder is higher than the other; how can I compensate for this?

Most people will find that they have one shoulder higher than the other. It may not be very obvious and you may well be surprised to find out that you too have this feature. Having one shoulder higher than the other is not, generally speaking, a bodily deformity. It arises simply as a consequence of everyday activities, such as carrying children or hanging bags from one shoulder.

Wearing a tight-fitting t-shirt or just your underwear, stand upright in front of a mirror, making sure your shoulders are relaxed, and have a good look at your shoulders. You will probably see that one shoulder is slightly higher. It may only be by a very small amount, but even this can effect the hang of a garment. If you ever wear a garment with a square neckline, the difference in height between your two shoulders may be more obvious.

For a pattern alteration to one side only, you need to make a copy of the existing front and back pattern pieces and then alter one copy for the high shoulder only using the instructions for broad shoulders in Question 98. Label one piece "right side up" and the other "wrong side up" as this is referring to the right and wrong sides of the fabric. Remember to only cut one of each out of the fabric and not a pair.

Question 101:
How do I change the shape of a neckline?

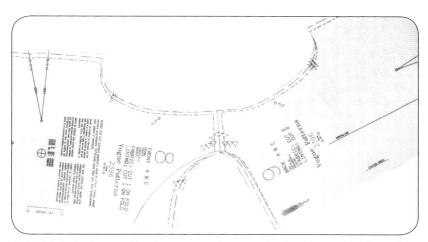

ABOVE Join the front and back pattern sections together in order to alter the neck.

Once you have found and perfected a blouse or dress pattern that fits well you obviously want to use it again but perhaps you want to add a new neckline for a change.

For example, you may want to change a simple round neck into a "V" neckline. Photocopy the front and back pieces of your round-neck pattern (so you don't have to cut up the original). Join the two pieces at stitching line (not the cutting line) of the shoulder seam. Lay out the joined-together pattern pieces flat. Draw your new neckline onto the front piece, tapering the line up to the shoulder seam. Use a curved ruler if necessary. Use a pencil at first so you can rub the line out if you aren't happy with it. If you've widened the neckline, remember to redraw the back neck too. Trim to the new cutting line. If you are unsure about the curve or depth of the "V" neckline, check by cutting just the front (on the fold) in calico and drape on yourself or your dummy. If you are happy with the neckline alteration, remember to alter the facings and linings.

Question 102:
The front of the neckline is gaping; how can I fix this?

With scooped or "V" necklines there is a danger of gaping, especially if you have a full bust.

For substantial amounts of gaping you need to lay the front pattern piece flat and draw two to three lines from the neck edge to the armhole. Cut along the lines, stopping within ¼ inch (5 mm) of the armhole, to leave a "hinge." Overlap the pattern at the neckline by no more than ¼ inch (5 mm) for each line. After the alteration you will need to redraw the cutting line around the neckline, and remember to alter any facings and linings too.

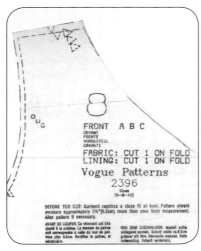

ABOVE Cut across the pattern from the neckline to the armhole and then overlap the cuts to reduce the fullness at the neck. Redraw the cutting line.

EXPERT TIP

❝ If you are working with a malleable fabric like wool, for example, you may find you can shrink small amounts of ease into the neckline when making, without altering the pattern. Always remember to measure and tape necklines when sewing as they have a habit of stretching. ❞

Question 103:
The back neck is gaping; how do I alter the pattern?

For a dress or shirt pattern there are a couple of options for addressing the issue of a gaping back neck.

The simplest method for a dress or shirt with a center back seam is to skim off the amount required from the back pattern neck edge tapering to nothing about 3⅜ inches (8 cm) further down the seam. If your pattern doesn't have a center back seam, it may be worth adding

one (see Question 96) to enable you to curve the seam very slightly into the back neck.

Another option is to add a small dart at the back neck edge with the dart measurement being the amount you would like to decrease. Angle the dart slightly toward the armhole and make the dart 2– 3⅜ inches (5–8 cm) long.

Question 104:
The front of the neckline is too loose; how do I decrease here?

A quick solution for altering a loose neckline, which requires only a small amount of reduction, is to take it in at the shoulder. Draw a line at the shoulder seam, starting ¼ to ⁵⁄₁₆ inch (5–7 mm) below the shoulder seam at the neck edge, tapering to nothing at the armhole edge. Trim to the new cutting line. Split between two shoulders, you can eliminate ⅜ to ⅝ inch (1–1.5 cm).

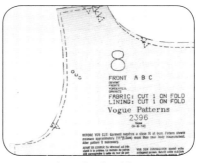

ABOVE Reduce the shoulder seam at the neckline to take in the looseness.

Question 105:
The neck is too tight; how can I increase it?

There are many different necklines with collars and lapels but for a basic understanding let's look at a simple round neck. If a neckline is too tight the pattern needs to be dropped down from the neck; as long as it feels comfortable on the body, it's a styling decision. A front neckline feels comfortable when it sits no higher than between the clavicle bones at the throat.

The first step is to join the front and back pattern pieces, as in Question 101. Lay out the pattern pieces and, starting at the center front, draw in a new neckline ⅜ inch (1 cm) from the cutting line. Using a curved ruler, curve this line around until it meets the shoulder. Continue drawing in a new curved neckline on the back pattern piece, dropping from the shoulder point toward the center back. Trim the pattern to the new cutting line.

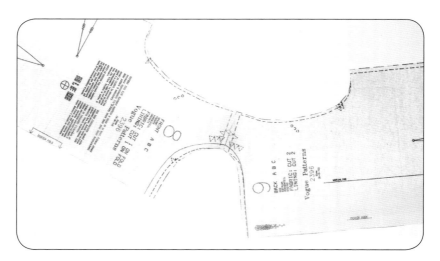

ABOVE Reduce tightness at the neck by increasing the space in the neckline on both the front and back pieces.

Question 106:
How do I add gathers to a neckline?

As discussed in Question 101, once you have found a good-fitting pattern, then neckline changes are always welcome.

If your pattern has a round or scooped neckline and you would like to add gathers, start by laying out your front pattern piece and work out where you want the gathers. If, for example, you want to add gathers 3 inches (7.5 cm) from the center front, on either side, first make a mark at the neckline at the 3 inches (7.5 cm) point. Draw two to three evenly spaced lines between the mark and the center front that run from the neck edge to the waist.

Cut along the lines and then spread the pattern pieces apart, tapering to nothing at the waist; the amount you spread the pattern apart depends on how much gathering you want and what fabric you are using. A fine fabric such as silk seems to absorb the gathers and will need a greater measurement on the pattern. Add extra paper behind the pattern to hold the alteration in place. Draw in the cutting line for the neck and trim the added paper accordingly. The neckline facings and linings will stay the same as the original neckline pattern.

Question 107:
How do I alter a pattern if I have a large bust and large tummy but narrow waist?

If you have a large bust only, then the alteration you need to follow is covered in Question 91. However, if you are also large over the abdomen, you need to increase the pattern in this area too.

Prepare and cut your pattern as you did for Question 91. Spread the pattern apart as you did to add space at the bust, but instead of tapering the pattern into the waist you need to spread it apart here too; this will give you more room over the tummy area. You will have to add extra paper underneath the pattern and redraw the cutting line.

If you are narrow at the waist, you need to reduce the waistline. Take off the desired amount by tapering the side seam on the front as well as the back pieces. Whatever the amount you need to reduce, remember to divide it by four since you will be reducing the two side seams on both the front and back.

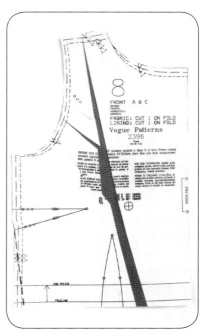

ABOVE If you've added to the pattern to give more room over your abdomen, remember to reduce the width at the waist if you are narrow at this point.

Question 108:
The positions of the buttonholes on my pattern aren't right for me; what should I do?

Making buttonholes and stitching on buttons are usually among the final tasks when you're making a garment. This is fortunate since it gives you a chance to try on the blouse or shirt to see if the buttonhole positions are in the correct place for you.

If the buttonholes marked on the pattern aren't right for you, then adjust their position—buttonholes should be placed in areas of stress. They should be positioned about ⅝ inch (1.5 cm) above and below the waistline and the same position around the bust area. If you have a full bust you may need to position buttons carefully to avoid the front opening gaping.

You may have noticed when you buy a shirt that the buttonholes are positioned so they run vertically down the center front but that the last buttonhole, just below the waist, is placed horizontally. This is a key stress point and a horizontal buttonhole stops the button from popping open. Horizontal buttonholes are normally placed about ¼ inch (5 mm) away from the center front and vertical buttonholes are positioned on the center front.

109 How can I increase the waistline?

110 How do I tighten the waistline?

111 How do I adjust the position of the waistline on a dress pattern?

112 How do I adjust the size of the waistband piece on a skirt pattern?

113 What is a "grown-on" waistband on a skirt?

114 How do I adapt a skirt pattern to have a grown-on waistband?

115 My tummy sticks out a bit; how do I compensate for this?

116 I'm pregnant; is it possible to adjust patterns to fit an expanding waistline?

117 How do I alter the pattern for a larger bottom?

118 I have a flat bottom; how do I adjust this area on the pattern?

119 How do I adjust for a swayback?

120 The skirt is too tight around the hips; how do I compensate for this?

121 I'm small around the hips; how can I decrease the hipline?

122 The pattern is too curved over the hips; can I change this?

123 How do I change the length of a skirt?

124 How do I shorten a skirt?

125 Can I use an A-line skirt pattern to cut out a skirt on the bias?

126 How do I ensure an even hemline?

127 How do I insert a pocket in a side seam?

6

ADJUSTING WAISTLINES AND SKIRTS

Question 109:
How can I increase the waistline?

To adjust the waistline and increase the pattern to fit, only alter the side seams and the darts. Don't make any alterations at the center front and center back seam; these are cut close to the grain line and if you add anything here, you will throw the pattern off the grain and this will affect the fit of the garment.

Decide how much you need to adjust the waistline by subtracting the waist measurement on the pattern from your actual waist measurement, remembering to add the ease at the same time (see Question 56). Divide this by four to get the amount you will add to each seam. Tape paper at each of the side seams and draw in the new cutting line, tapering the line down for 1¼–1½ inches (3–4 cm) to meet the original seam. Use a curved ruler to draw in the curve of the hip. Trim the paper to the new cutting line.

To avoid adding too much at the side seam and risk distorting the hipline, you can also reduce the darts at the waistline. Using a ruler, draw straight lines inside the existing dart lines to make new darts. Remember to transfer this information to your fabric pieces.

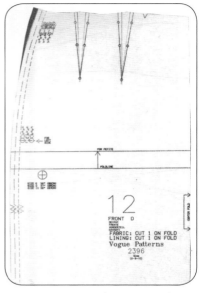

ABOVE To increase the space you have in the waist of a skirt you can add a bit extra at the side seam and reduce the width of the darts.

Adjusting Waistlines and Skirts

Question 110:
How do I tighten the waistline?

If you feel that the hip area fits on the skirt but the waist is too loose and causing the skirt to drop down, then a simple alteration on the pattern can help.

The following pattern alteration is successful when decreasing by up to 2 inches (5 cm); much more than that will distort the pattern. Measure the waistline on the pattern and your waist measurement plus ease and the difference is the amount you need to decrease. Divide this by four to get the amount you will deduct from each side seam. Lay out the front and back patterns and draw in a new cutting line at the hip, taking off the amount required and gently tapering to nothing at the side seam 2¼–3½ inches (6–8 cm) below the waist. Use a curved ruler to help you draw in the new cutting line. Trim the pattern to this line.

Depending on the amount you need to deduct, you can also adjust the dart measurement at the waist. Draw in new dart lines outside the existing ones so that you take in more fabric at the waist during construction. Transfer the new dart to the fabric piece when cut out.

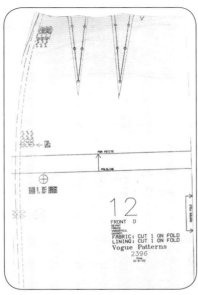

ABOVE When you adjust a skirt pattern at the waistline, remember to make the same adjustments on both front and back pieces.

Question 111:
How do I adjust the position of the waistline on a dress pattern?

If you are tall or short, you will find buying dresses is a bit hit and miss, as it often appears that either the hips feel tight if you are tall or there is an excess of fabric somewhere above the waist if you are short. This is because the waistline is not in the correct position for your body shape. When you make your own clothes there is a basic alteration which will solve the problem.

Lay out the front and back dress patterns and measure from the back neck or shoulder line to waist and compare with your body measurements. Almost all commercial patterns have a "lengthen and shorten here" line at the waist. This is where you either fold the pattern toward the back neck to shorten the measurement, or where you cut through the pattern and tape paper underneath to increase the measurement. Always remember to alter both the back and front patterns.

RIGHT If you are tall, cut the pattern at the "lengthen here" line and add some paper to get the desired new length.

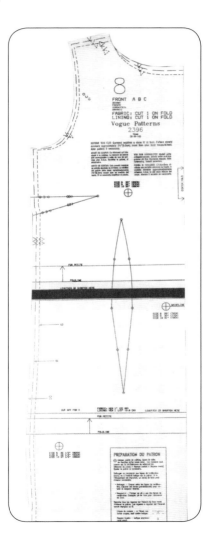

Adjusting Waistlines and Skirts

Question 112:
How do I adjust the size of the waistband piece on a skirt pattern?

If you are altering a skirt at the waist and if that skirt has a separate waistband, you will also need to increase or decrease the measurement of the waistband.

The easiest way to increase the waistband is to cut through the pattern at the side seams and add the extra measurement here. Divide the total you want to increase in half, and then add this at each of the side seams. For example, if your total adjustment is 1½ inches (4 cm) add ¾ inch (2 cm) to the waistband at the two side seam points. Add new paper sections of the right amount and tape everything together. Make sure that you trim the new paper to the cutting line.

To decrease the waistband you can simply fold the pattern at the side seams by the required amount; remember to divide that amount in half, between the two seams.

After altering your waistband you may need to check that the notches match between your waistband and skirt pattern, especially if you have adjusted the darts on the skirt. The notches will enable you to attach the waistband to the skirt pattern easily and accurately.

Question 113:
What is a "grown-on" waistband on a skirt?

A "grown-on" waistband on a skirt is when there is no visible waistband and the skirt is in one piece from the hem to the waist edge. Skirts can be flattering with a grown-on waistband and this can be an interesting design feature.

Although there appears to be no waistband, the waistline on this style of skirt is finished—the waist area is supported by a front and a back facing inside the skirt. These facings follow the shape of the front and back pattern pieces. The facing pattern pieces will be marked with notches, grain lines, and seam allowances that correspond to the rest of the skirt pattern.

Facings are always fused to give the same support that a "normal" waistband would have. Contrasting fabrics and colors can be used on facings to give a garment an individual look.

LEFT Many different skirt styles can be made with a grown-on waistband.

Question 114:
How do I adapt a skirt pattern to have a grown-on waistband?

Adapting a skirt pattern for a grown-on waistband is relatively simple. The key to success is to be methodical in your processes.

Lay out the front and back skirt pattern pieces and measure the waist, excluding all darts and allowances. Check that the measurement is the same as yours, allowing for ease (see Question 56). Start with the front pattern. Tape paper along the top of the waistband and overlap near the side seam. Decide on how deep you want the waistband and then draw a line across the paper, this distance from the waist of the skirt.

Draw a line up from the edge of each dart perpendicular to and meeting this new line. Extend the side seam up to the new line. Then draw a new side-seam line, angled away from the first by about $\frac{3}{8}$ inch (1 cm). Fold away the darts on the front and back skirt and check the line of the new "grown-on" waistband and redraw areas if necessary. When you cut out the fabric, transfer any markings to the fabric and mark where you want to turn under the waistband.

To make a facing for the front and back skirt, fold away the darts on the front pattern and place on top of paper and trace the shape of the front facing, extending down to the waistline and adding your seam allowance. Follow the same process for the back facing, then place the back and front together, match the side seams, and check that you have gentle curves.

Question 115:
My tummy sticks out a bit; how do I compensate for this?

You may find if you have a bit of a tummy that skirts, dresses, and tops lift at the hem, and don't hang perpendicular to the floor.

Lay out your front pattern piece and draw a line from the mid-shoulder to the bottom of the pattern. Draw another line across the center of the dart. Draw a line from the end of the dart perpendicular to the center front. Cut along the vertical line, stopping within ¼ inch (5 mm) of the shoulder, to leave a "hinge." Cut along the dart and horizontal line.

Spread the pattern apart vertically with about ⅝ inch (1.5 cm) space at the hem. Avoid any alterations to the shoulder by tapering to nothing. Tape paper under the pattern. Redraw the bottom cutting line and trim. Add ⅝–1 inch (1.5–2.5 cm) horizontally and tape in some paper.

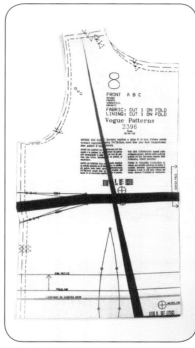

ABOVE To increase space at the waistline over the tummy, you need to make adjustments to the bodice.

Question 116:
I'm pregnant; is it possible to adjust patterns to fit an expanding waistline?

The main criteria for maternity clothes is comfort and room for an expanding bump.

For dresses and tops, follow the pattern alteration in Question 115, but add more horizontally from the side seam to the center front.

If you would like to adapt a skirt pattern, one solution is to replace the waistband and part of the skirt pattern with a jersey or lycra fabric.

To alter a skirt pattern for this, lay out the front piece and mark the lowest point under your baby bump on the center front. Draw in a curved yoke shape up to the waistline, finishing 4–6 inches (10–15 cm) from the side seams. Draw another line inside this curved line for the seam allowance. Cut out the shape. Use this cut out piece as the pattern for the jersey insert, adding a seam allowance around the curved bottom edge. Depending on the stretch of the jersey you might be able to ignore the front darts; if not, eliminate them by folding out the darts on the pattern.

Use the jersey on the double by having a fold line at the top edge of the skirt; get rid of the seam allowance before making the fold line and remember to add seam allowances at the bottom of the curve. The back skirt stays as the original pattern. Ideally you have a grown-on waistband with facings that attach at the side seam.

Question 117:
How do I alter the pattern for a larger bottom?

One of the telltale signs of having a large bottom is that the skirt wrinkles and rides up at the back, causing the hemline to lift and the side seams to swing backward.

There are two steps for altering the skirt pattern, depending on where you feel you need more room. First, to stop the back hem from rising, lay out the back pattern and draw a line from the center back to the side seam, 6–7 inches (15–18 cm) below the waistline, at the fullest part of the thighs or high hip. Cut through the line stopping within ¼ inch (5 mm) of the side seam, to leave a "hinge." Spread open to the amount needed and tape some paper under the pattern; carefully redraw the center back line.

The second step will give you more room over the bottom as well as stopping the side seams from swaying toward the back. Lay out the back pattern and draw vertical lines through the center of the waist darts (only one line is needed if there is only one dart) to the hem. Cut along the lines, stopping within ¼ inch (5 mm) of the hem, to leave a "hinge." Spread the pattern open

to the amount you need, tapering to nothing at the hem. Tape paper under the openings. Remember to split the measurement between the two back pieces. To keep the waistline the same measurement make bigger darts to compensate.

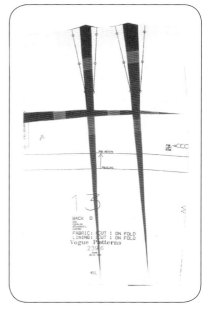

ABOVE There are two ways to add space for a large bottom; you may need to combine both.

Question 118:
I have a flat bottom; how do I adjust this area on the pattern?

If you have a small or flat bottom, skirts often seem to fit at the hip but at the back of the skirt the fabric hangs in folds and looks as though it's too big. The pattern alteration for this is simple and it helps to reduce the excess fabric around the seat, without altering the fit over the hip.

Lay out your back pattern piece and draw a vertical line through the center of each waist dart to the hem. Cut along the lines, stopping within ¼ inch (5 mm) of the hem, to leave a "hinge." Divide the amount you wish to take out by the number of darts; so if you have two darts in the back pattern piece and you will be cutting out two pieces of fabric with that pattern, you need to divide the amount by four. Overlap the pattern at the waistline where you have cut the lines by the desired amount, so that the

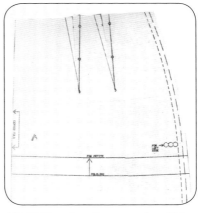

ABOVE To reduce the excess in a skirt over a flat bottom, take the desired amount out at the darts, tapering down over the length of the skirt.

reduction tapers down to the hem. Tape the alteration in place. You may have to redraw the dart, which will have reduced slightly. However, this is desirable, as less shaping is important if you have a flat bottom.

Question 119:
How do I adjust for a swayback?

You might find when wearing skirts or pants, horizontal folds or wrinkles appear in the small of your back between the waist and hip; this usually indicates that you have a swayback. Most women are full in the bottom and this is a common feature. To help eradicate the folds, the same alteration can be carried out on skirts, dresses, and pants.

Lay out the back pattern and draw a horizontal line from the center back to the side seam, 2–3¼ inches (5–8 cm) below the waistline. Cut through the line stopping within ¼ inch (5 mm) of the side seam, to leave a "hinge." Overlap the pattern at the center back by the required amount, usually ⅜–¾ inch (1–2 cm). Redraw the center-back cutting line, which you might have to straighten and possibly alter darts and the side seam. Keep the grain line as the original line, redrawing if necessary.

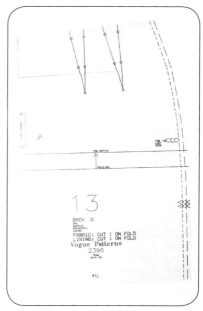

ABOVE To correct for a swayback you need to take out the excess in the back of the skirt.

Question 120:
The skirt is too tight around the hips; how do I compensate for this?

There's nothing worse than wearing a skirt that's too tight over the hips. The skirt rides up and unsightly creases appear across the front skirt as the fabric strains.

Measure your pattern across the hips and then subtract this from your hip measurement. Add any ease to this measurement (see Question 56) to find out how much you need to add. The extra is added at the side seams so divide the amount equally by four.

Lay out the front pattern and tape paper under the side seam. Draw in a new hipline with your desired increase at the fullest point of the hip, and tapering to nothing at the waist. Taper to nothing at the hem if you are altering a pencil skirt, but draw the line straight down for a straight skirt, or at an angle for an A-line skirt. Use a curved ruler to draw in any curves. Trim the added paper to the new cutting line. Repeat on the back pattern, making sure that the hip curve is the same as on the front piece (you could use the front piece as a template).

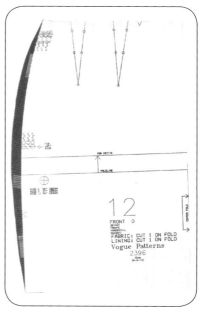

ABOVE If you create a new cutting line at the side seam of your skirt which curves outward, you should be able to avoid tightness over the hips.

Question 121:
I'm small around the hips; how can I decrease the hipline?

If you are lucky enough to have small hips, you may find that skirts tend to look loose around this area and the side seams appear to drop. A simple pattern alteration will remedy the problem and make the fabric lie flat over the body.

Measure the pattern and subtract your hip measurement, remembering to include any ease (see Question 56). This is the amount you need to decrease at the hip. The amount is deducted at the side seams, so divide it by four.

Lay out the front pattern and draw in a new cutting line along the side seam, starting at the waist the required amount in from the side. Taper to nothing at the hem if you want to keep the original hem circumference, or reduce the side seam at the hem also for a narrower style skirt. Trim the pattern to the new cutting line. Repeat with the back pattern piece.

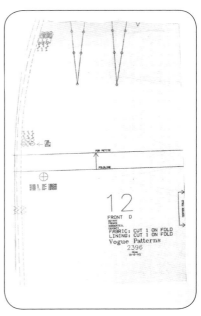

ABOVE To reduce a skirt pattern at the hip, trim a little off at the side seams on both front and back pattern pieces.

Question 122:
The pattern is too curved over the hips; can I change this?

If the skirt pattern generally fits well but the fabric pokes out a bit at the hip, this can be easily altered.

Work out the required amount to be taken off the curve. Lay out the front skirt pattern and draw the new hip shape, much as you did for Question 121, but start from nothing at the waist and taper to nothing at

the hip; you do not want to reduce the pattern at any other point. Trim the pattern to the new cutting line. Repeat on the back pattern. Check that everything matches by placing the sides seams together on the front and back pattern pieces and confirm that the notches match.

Question 123:
How do I change the length of a skirt?

The beauty of making your own clothes is being able to make skirts and dresses the right length for you and not having to put up with a garment that is too long or short.

Changing the length of a skirt is a simple alteration. If you look at the pattern you will see a line marked across it, labeled "lengthen or shorten here." To lengthen a skirt, cut across this line and insert extra paper to the desired depth.

When altering the length of a skirt, remember to add or subtract the same amount on both the front and back pattern pieces. Also, if you are adding or subtracting more than 2 inches (5 cm) try to do it in more than one place over the length of the skirt.

Question 124:
How do I shorten a skirt?

To shorten a skirt pattern, start by laying out the front pattern piece and find the line labeled "shorten or lengthen here." Simply fold the pattern along this line to reduce the length of the skirt.

If you need to shorten the skirt by more than 2 inches (5 cm), then you should shorten the pattern in two places; this equal distribution will keep the correct pattern proportion. Use the line marked on the pattern as your first line, and then draw another horizontal line 4–6 inches (10–15 cm) above or below the first. Take out the amount you want to reduce by folding the pattern at both lines. After completing the pattern alteration, redraw the cutting line at the side seam if necessary. Repeat the process on the back pattern piece. Make sure the front and back pattern pieces are the same length before you cut out your fabric.

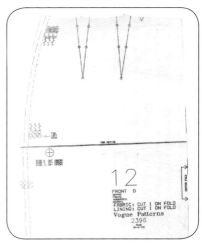

ABOVE Commercial skirt, dress, and pants patterns feature a convenient marked line to indicate the ideal place to lengthen or shorten.

Question 125:
Can I use an A-line skirt pattern to cut out a skirt on the bias?

With a little bit of tweaking, you can use an A-line skirt pattern to cut out a skirt on the bias. This can give a garment a totally different look; see Question 71.

To use an A-line skirt pattern on the bias, it's necessary to change the direction of the grain line on each pattern piece. Place your ruler on the marked straight grain line and then move it so that it lies at a 45-degree angle to the grain line. You may need to use a suitable measuring tool to get the angle right (some design rulers and patternmasters feature angled lines). Draw in the new grain line. Then, when you place the pattern pieces on your fabric, match the new grain line to the selvedge (see Question 77). You will not be able to follow the original layout plans for your pattern.

When cutting an A-line skirt on the bias, check the nap of the fabric before cutting to see what the visual effect will be. If you are cutting a corduroy or striped fabric, you may want to add a center front seam and achieve a chevron effect.

Question 126:
How do I ensure an even hemline?

There are many reasons why you might end up with an uneven hemline. This chapter has addressed problems that could be responsible for a rising hem, such as a big bottom, tightness over the hips, and a big tummy. However, once you have cut out and made a garment, you need to know how to fix an uneven hem.

The easiest way to ensure a level hem is to try on the unhemmed garment and, with the help of a friend, measure the distance from the floor to the required hem length. This can be done with a tape measure but it works more successfully with a solid ruler or a T-square. Measure all the way around the hem, marking with pins as you go. When you have finished, take off the garment and lay it flat to check the pinned line. Make sure you can tell where the hemline is by the pins, and draw it in with tailor's chalk if necessary. Add on your allowance for a hem and then trim off the excess.

Question 127:
How do I insert a pocket in a side seam?

If you have a skirt, pants, or dress pattern and you would like to add a functional pocket to the side seam, it's a simple pattern addition.

Lay out the back pattern piece and decide where on the side seam you would like your pocket to sit. The back part of the pocket is "grown-on" at the side seam, which means there is no separate piece of fabric cut. It is usually positioned about 2 inches (5 cm) below the waistline. The shape of the pocket is up to you; either roughly draw around your hand in a downward slope or find a pocket to copy from another pattern. Simply attach the pocket pattern piece to the side seam of the back pattern.

On the front pattern you need to add a small facing to the side seam. Then cut out a separate piece of fabric for the front of the pocket; stitch it to the facing. (The front pocket piece is sometimes made from lining fabric to reduce the bulk caused by so many layers.) Remember to check that both the front and back pockets match, as it can be confusing with facings and added seam allowances.

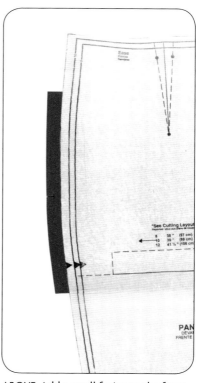

ABOVE Add a small facing to the front pattern piece where you want to attach the pocket.

128 What is a good-fitting sleeve?

129 What can I do if the armhole is tight?

130 How do you alter the pattern for large upper arms?

131 How do I get more room on the sleeve cap only?

132 How do you lengthen a sleeve?

133 How do you shorten a sleeve?

134 I want to omit the sleeves on a pattern; how do I adjust the armhole?

135 For a sleeveless option, how do I make an armhole facing?

136 Can I add sleeves to a sleeveless dress pattern?

137 What do I do if the back of the armhole is gaping on a sleeveless top?

138 How do I take out gathers on a sleeve?

139 I love the dress but it has straight sleeves and I want puff sleeves; how do I change this?

140 How do I make a flared sleeve?

141 How do I make the wrists narrower?

142 How do I make the pattern wider at the wrist?

143 How do I create a gathered wrist line?

144 I want to create a shaped cuff at the wrist; how do I do this?

ADJUSTING SLEEVES
AND ARMHOLES

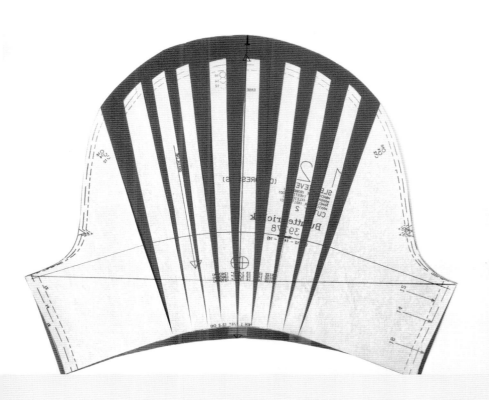

Question 128:
What is a good-fitting sleeve?

If you stand with your arms by your side, they are naturally slightly bent at the elbows. There is also an inclination for your arms to hang slightly forward. This is worth remembering when you are fitting sleeves; the sleeves shouldn't be straight tubes, they need to be shaped to conform with the shape and natural hang of your arms.

A good-fitting sleeve should fit the arm and shoulder smoothly and allow the arm to move easily without straining. When the sleeve is correctly balanced the lengthwise grain will hang straight from the shoulder point and be perpendicular to the floor and the crosswise grain will be parallel to the floor. A term often used to describe the fit of a sleeve is "pitch," this refers to which direction the sleeve is leaning—either to the back or the front. The pitch alters the way the sleeve hangs. If the sleeve appears to be dragging at the front or at the back, you can modify the pitch of the sleeve cap by moving the notches that tell you where to position the sleeve on the bodice. At the armhole edge of the bodice, move the position of the notches slightly, ¼ inch (5 mm), either forward or backward.

Question 129:
What can I do if the armhole is tight?

Sleeves can be troublesome areas to alter, as it's necessary to have a certain amount of ease for movement and sometimes it's confusing to know which area to let out and what to take in. If the armhole feels tight under the arm, the solution is to add to both the bodice armhole and the sleeve.

Lay out the front pattern and draw a horizontal line from the armhole to the center front. Cut through the line. Put some paper underneath the pattern and then spread the pattern apart by the amount needed, up to ¾ inch (2 cm). Tape the paper in place and then redraw the cutting line at armhole and center front. Trim the extra paper to the cutting line. Follow the same procedure for the back pattern, making sure you add the same amount. When you've made the alteration, check that the front and back pattern pieces match.

Lay out the sleeve pattern and draw a horizontal line through the sleeve head. Draw the line in a position that corresponds with the one you drew on the front and back pieces—use the notches on the pattern to guide you. Cut through the line. Put some paper underneath the pattern and then spread the pattern apart by the same amount you added on the bodice. Tape the paper in place and then redraw the cutting line and check that the notches on all pieces match.

ABOVE To put more room in the armhole increase the depth of the bodice first.

EXPERT TIP

❝ The measurement of the armhole edge of the sleeve is always bigger than the front and back armhole measurement. Depending on your chosen fabric (wool absorbs more ease than cotton or silk) there should be at least ⅝ inch (1.5cm) ease on either side of the center notch on the sleeve head. ❞

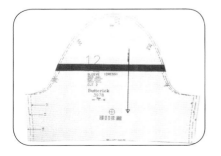

LEFT You then need to increase the depth of the sleeve head.

Question 130:
How do you alter the pattern for large upper arms?

If a sleeve feels tight or if you struggle to get your arm into a sleeve, then the pattern is too tight. Once you have worked out where the sleeve feels uncomfortable you can begin to alter the pattern.

Draw a vertical line down the pattern to divide the sleeve in half lengthways (you may be able to follow the grain line guide marked on the pattern). Draw a horizontal line across the sleeve, across the point where you want to add some fullness. Cut along the vertical line to cut the pattern in two. Cut along each horizontal line, stopping within ¼ inch (5 mm) of the side seam, to leave a "hinge." Place the pattern flat on a piece of paper. Spread the pattern apart along the vertical line to the amount required at the upper arm area; this will automatically make the horizontal lines overlap. Tape the paper in place.

Measure the amount eliminated at the overlapping horizontal line. Tape a piece of paper to the top of the sleeve pattern and make a mark this amount from the top of the sleeve. Draw in a new cutting line, following the shape of the sleeve

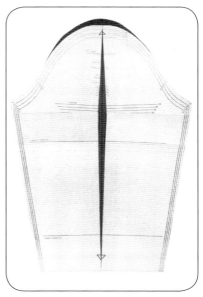

ABOVE To increase at the upper arms you need to make both vertical and horizontal cuts in the pattern, then open out the pattern at the point where the cut lines bisect.

head and tapering to nothing at the sides. This will return the sleeve to its original length. Trim to the new cutting line. Redraw the grain line and remember to check that the notches match between the sleeve and the armhole.

Question 131:
How do I get more room on the sleeve cap only?

If your bodice is generally a good fit but feels and looks just a little tight around the sleeve cap and across the bodice front, there is an easy alteration you can do that doesn't affect the bodice piece.

Lay out the sleeve pattern and draw a vertical line down the pattern to divide the sleeve in half lengthways (see Question 130). Cut along the line. Place paper underneath the pattern and spread it open to the amount needed; either continue the same amount throughout the pattern or taper to nothing at the sleeve hem. Tape the paper in place and redraw the cutting line at the sleeve head. Trim to the new cutting line. Redraw the grain line and any notches.

This method works if you are only adding up to ¾ inch (2 cm). Any more and you won't be able to ease the sleeve into the bodice.

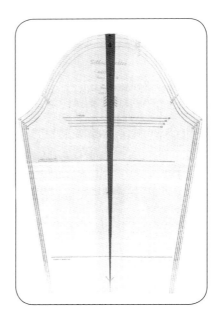

RIGHT If you want to increase the very top of the sleeve only—the sleeve head—simply cut the sleeve in half lengthwise and open it out at the top.

Question 132:
How do you lengthen a sleeve?

Commercial patterns are marked with helpful "lengthening and shortening" lines. Cut the pattern in two at the lengthening line, place paper underneath, and then spread the pattern apart to your required amount. Use the existing grain line as a guide to help you keep the two parts of the sleeve lined up correctly. Tape the paper in place and redraw the grain line and cutting lines. Don't add more than ¾ inch (2 cm) at one point or you will lose some of the proportion of the sleeve. If you need to add more, lengthen at two points, one above and one below the elbow.

RIGHT Lengthen the sleeve in two places if you need to add more than ¾ inch (2 cm).

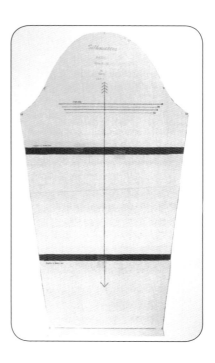

Question 133:
How do you shorten a sleeve?

Shortening a commercial sleeve pattern is as simple as lengthening it since you have the "lengthening and shortening" line to guide you.

Simply locate this line and then fold the pattern piece up to the required amount. You can use the grain line marking printed on the pattern to make sure you keep the sleeve straight and even.

When shortening a sleeve don't subtract more than ¾ inch (2 cm) at any one point. If you do, the sleeve will not have the same proportion and won't hang as well. You need to disperse the amount being deducted between two points, one above and one below the elbow. Once you have folded the pattern, you may need to redraw the cutting lines at the sleeve side seam.

RIGHT Fold the pattern along the marked lines to shorten it. Do this in two places if you need to lose more than ¾ inch (2 cm).

Question 134:
I want to omit the sleeves on a pattern; how do I adjust the armhole?

If you decide not to use the sleeves on a particular pattern, you may find the armhole needs reshaping. Everyone is different and comfort under the armhole is crucial, so if you are altering significantly, it's worth making a quick toile, so you can see exactly how much you need to alter the pattern.

Lay out the front and back pieces and bring them together so they meet at the side seam, matching up the stitching line, not the cutting line. Decide if you want to raise or lower the armhole; bear in mind that you need to have at least ¾ inch (2 cm) above the bra. Redraw the curve of the armhole to your desired shape—you will need to add paper if you are raising the armhole.

If you look at the original armhole on the front and back patterns, you'll see the armhole curve on the front is more acute than on the back. Mimic this difference with your new armhole.

Question 135:
For a sleeveless option, how do I make an armhole facing?

Once you have redrawn the armhole for a sleeveless option (see Question 134), you will need to finish off the armhole edges with a facing. You need two facings, one for the front and one for the back.

Photocopy both your front and back pattern pieces; you can then cut these up to make patterns for the facings. (If you don't have access to a photocopier, you can always trace around the pattern onto a separate piece of paper and cut the new pattern out of this.) Lay out the front pattern and make a mark on the center front 3¼–4 inches (8–10 cm) below the neckline. Make another mark on the side seam below the armhole. Starting at the side seam, draw a line following the curve of the armhole to about half way up the armhole. Then take the line across the pattern to meet the mark at the center front. Keep the line curving and fluid. Repeat on the back pattern. Cut along your drawn

lines to create the facing patterns. If your original pattern has a shoulder dart, mark it on the facing pattern but eliminate it when you cut out the fabric for the facings by folding it away. Before cutting out, match the side seams and check that the curve is smooth. It's worth remembering that you will either attach a lining to this curve or overlock it, so try to make it as sewing-machine friendly as possible.

RIGHT Use a photocopy of your original pattern and draw the desired facing onto that before cutting out to create a new pattern.

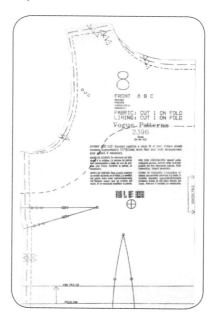

Question 136:
Can I add sleeves to a sleeveless dress pattern?

In an ideal world, you would have one or two patterns that fit you beautifully, and which you could add to or remove various design features as and when you wish. If you have found that perfect sleeveless dress pattern, then you should hang onto it, since you can adapt it by putting in sleeves.

To do this, you will be "borrowing" a sleeve pattern from another garment. Try and pick one that you know fits you and in a style that will suit the sleeveless dress you are adapting.

Roughly measure the armhole of the sleeveless dress and then measure the sleeve head of the borrowed pattern. To make life easier, they should be the right size for each other—the sleeve head will be about 1¼ inches (3 cm) more than the armhole (see Expert Tip on Question 129). If they don't match, then try and find a sleeve pattern that does. The shoulder seam of

the pattern from which you are borrowing the sleeve should be at the same angle as the shoulder seam on the sleeveless dress. If not, you will have to redraw the shoulder seam on the sleeveless-dress pattern to match, which may also mean adjusting the armhole.

Photocopy the front and back bodice pieces of your sleeveless pattern—this is so you don't have to cut up that treasured good-fitting pattern! Lay out the front bodice piece for your sleeveless dress and then place the bodice piece of the "borrowed" pattern over the top. Trace around the armhole and shoulder line to create a new cutting line; trim the photocopied sleeveless pattern. The armhole and shoulder will now fit the borrowed sleeve pattern. Repeat with the back bodice piece. Transfer all notches from the borrowed pattern to the new sleeveless pattern and check that they still match.

Question 137:
What do I do if the back of the armhole is gaping on a sleeveless top?

If the armhole on the back pattern is gaping slightly, this can be easily eliminated with a small alteration.

Lay out the back pattern and draw a horizontal line from the armhole to the center back. Cut along this line, stopping within ¼ inch (5 mm) of the shoulder, to leave a "hinge." Overlap this cut line at the armhole to remove the excess amount. Tape down the overlap and redraw the cutting lines. Remember to do the same alteration on the pattern for the armhole facing.

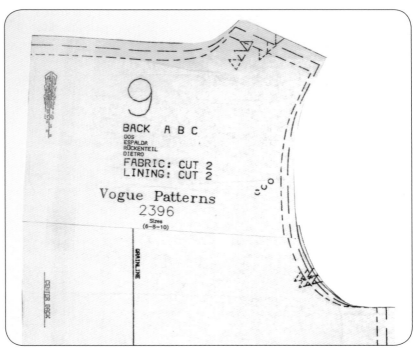

9

BACK A B C
DOS
ESPALDA
RÜCKENTEIL
DIETRO
FABRIC: CUT 2
LINING: CUT 2

Vogue Patterns
2396
Sizes
(6–8–10)

ABOVE To eliminate a gaping armhole at the back, cut across the pattern at the armhole and then overlap the cut at the armhole edge; tape in place.

Question 138:
How do I take out gathers on a sleeve?

Lay out the sleeve pattern and draw four to six vertical lines, so you have two to three lines on either side of the shoulder notch and the central grain line. Don't draw the lines beyond the back and front notches to retain the underarm fit.

Cut through the vertical lines, stopping within ¼ inch (5 mm) of the hem, to leave a "hinge." Start to evenly overlap the lines at the sleeve head to reduce by the required amount. Pin or weigh down the overlaps, then measure the sleeve head to check that it fits the armhole opening. The sleeve head should be about 1¼ inches (3 cm) bigger than the armhole opening for ease, and this may take a little tweaking until it's correct. Redraw the sleeve head, dropping the cutting line by about 1 inch (2.5 cm). Check that the notches on the front and back sleeve align with the bodice. Redraw the cutting line on the sleeve hem.

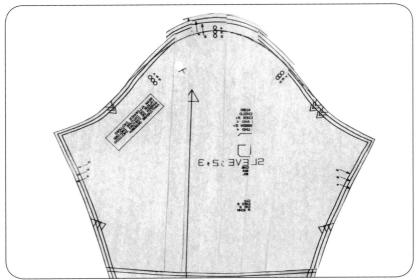

ABOVE When you've reduced the amount at the top of the sleeve head, redraw the cutting line, making it about 1 inch (2.5 cm) below the top edge.

Question 139:
I love the dress but it has straight sleeves and I want puff sleeves; how do I change this?

Adding fullness to a sleeve pattern may seem like a daunting prospect but all it takes is a little time and a few sheets of extra paper.

To make the puff of the sleeve sit correctly on the edge of the shoulder, you need to make a small adjustment to the bodice where you would attach the sleeve. Lay out the front pattern piece and trim off ⅜ inch (1 cm) at the armhole edge of the shoulder, tapering to

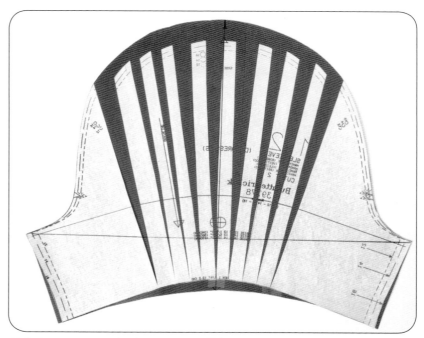

ABOVE To turn a straight sleeve into a puff sleeve you need add an even amount across the top of the sleeve.

nothing along the armhole edge. Repeat with the back pattern. This small pattern tweak helps give more support to the gathers of the sleeve and gives a better finish.

Lay out the sleeve head and draw six to nine vertical lines from the sleeve head to the hem, spacing them evenly between the notches that mark the front and back, so you retain the underarm sleeve fit.

Draw a straight horizontal line across the pattern at the widest part; it should cross the vertical grain line at right angles.

Cut through the vertical lines, stopping within ¼ inch (5 mm) of the hem, to leave a "hinge." Place extra paper under the whole pattern (you may have to tape several sheets together to get a large enough piece). Fan out the sleeve until you get the fullness you want. Try and get the spacing between the vertical lines you have cut as even as possible. It may take a few tweaks to get this just right.

When you are happy with the result, tape the sleeve pattern down into its new position on the paper.

Mark a point about 1 inch (2.5 cm) above the top-center point of the sleeve. Redraw the curve of the sleeve head between this point and the uncut parts of the sleeve. Use a curved ruler. Trim the paper to this new cutting line. Mark a new center notch at the top of the sleeve and redraw the grain line.

To check that the grain line is in the right position, draw a new horizontal line across the pattern at the widest part. If this crosses the grain line at right angles, the grain line is in the right position. The first horizontal line you drew should now be curved. Check that the curve is even on both sides of the grain line.

The sleeve hem will be slightly curved now and will need tightening to your arm measurement. Draw in a little extra at the hem and at the side seams at the hem edge. Trim the paper to the new cutting line. A hem facing will also be needed, as a normal hem won't fold if the curve is too acute.

Question 140:
How do I make a flared sleeve?

With a basic set-in sleeve it is possible to adapt it to a variety of different sleeve styles. Creating a sleeve that flares from the elbow is a straightforward alteration.

Lay out the sleeve pattern and mark the elbow area with a horizontal line running across the sleeve. Now mark four to seven vertical lines from this line to the hem. Cut across the horizontal line to divide the pattern into two parts. Cut through the vertical lines on the bottom half of the sleeve pattern, stopping within ¼ inch (5 mm) of the hem, to leave a "hinge." Place extra paper under the whole pattern (you may have to tape several sheets together to get a large enough piece). Fan out the bottom part of the sleeve until you get the flare you want. Tape the adjusted pattern to the paper. Redraw the side seams and the curve of the hem. Trim the paper to the new cutting line. Redraw the original grain line and check that both the sleeve seams match in length.

ABOVE When you've finished your alteration, measure both side seams to make sure they still match.

Question 141:
How do I make the wrists narrower?

If you want to make the wrist narrower by only a small amount—no more than 1¼ inches (3 cm)—this is easily reduced at the sleeve side seams. Work out how much you want to loose and divide this in two. Make a mark on the hemline this far in from the left side seam. Draw a line from this point to about 4 inches (10 cm) up the side seam, tapering to nothing. Repeat on the right-hand side of the sleeve. Trim both sides to the new cutting lines.

If you want to narrow the wrists more significantly, lay out your sleeve pattern and mark a horizontal line below the elbow area across the sleeve pattern. Now mark three to four vertical lines from this line to the hem. Cut across the horizontal line to divide the pattern into two parts. Starting at the hem edge, cut through the vertical lines on the bottom half of the sleeve pattern, stopping within ¼ inch (5 mm) of the top edge, to leave a "hinge." Place some paper under the pattern. Overlap the pieces at the wrist to reduce the pattern to your desired amount.

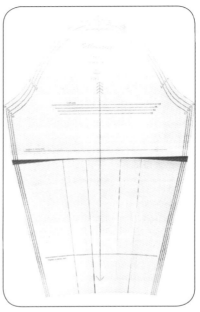

ABOVE To take a lot out of the wrist you need to evenly space your reductions over the width of the sleeve.

Tape the altered pattern to the paper. Redraw any cutting lines, smooth off any pronounced curves, and then trim the extra paper to the cutting lines. Check that the sleeve seams match in length.

Question 142:
How do I make the pattern wider at the wrist?

Altering the wrist width by small amounts, up to about 1¼ inches (3 cm), can be achieved by adding at the hem on the sleeve seams. Tape some paper under both sides of the sleeve pattern. Work out how much you want to add and divide this in two. Draw a line this far from the side seam to a point about 4 inches (10 cm) up the side seam, tapering to nothing. Repeat on the right-hand side of the sleeve. Trim off the extra paper to the new cutting lines.

If you would like the wrist area to be wider and generally fuller, follow the instructions in Question 140 for making a flared sleeve, but draw the horizontal line across the sleeve lower than the elbow. This alteration will give you an all-around fullness to the wrist area.

Question 143:
How do I create a gathered wrist line?

To create a gathered wrist line is simply a matter of adding fullness to the sleeve pattern and then gathering up the fabric when you make the garment. The gathering could be held in with various different methods such as elastic, drawstring, or a cuff.

Lay out your sleeve pattern and draw three to four evenly spaced vertical lines across the center of the sleeve head. Starting at the hem edge, cut through the vertical lines, stopping within ¼ inch (5 mm) of the sleeve head to leave a "hinge." Place some paper under the pattern. Fan the pattern open at the hem to the desired amount of fullness. Tape the altered pattern to the paper. Redraw any cutting lines, redraw the original grain line, and then trim the extra paper to the cutting lines. Check that the sleeve seams match in length.

Question 144:
I want to create a shaped cuff at the wrist; how do I do this?

If you want, it is possible to alter the style of your pattern's cuffs by shaping the edges. Before you begin, look at the cuff pattern piece. If it says "Cut 2" on it, and if you are meant to place the top edge of the cuff on the fold of the fabric to cut out, you will have to add a seam allowance. You won't be able to fold the fabric in half to form the cuff if it has curved corners, so you have to cut out four pieces of fabric, two for each cuff, and stitch them wrong sides together (with interfacing) before turning to the right side.

Tape some extra paper to the top edge of the cuff pattern; the top edge is the one not marked with any notches. Draw a line across the paper ⅝ inch (1.5 cm) from the top edge of the cuff (or whatever your pattern's seam allowance is). Extend the side seams.

Using a curved ruler, round off the corners at the top edge. If the original cuff pattern required you to "Cut 4" pieces, then you can simply round off the corners on the pattern, rather than add the extra paper for the allowance.

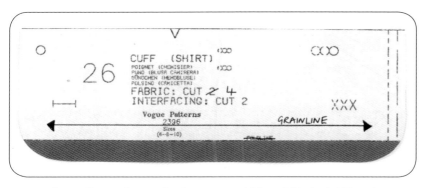

ABOVE Plain cuffs are often made of one piece of fabric, folded in half lengthwise. If you shape the corners of the cuff, you won't be able to cut it out of just one piece. Each cuff will need to be made up of two pieces of fabric and one piece of interfacing. To keep the cuff the same depth, you will have to add an allowance to the top edge.

145 How can I tell if the pants will fit?

146 What is the crotch length and how do I measure it?

147 How do I increase the crotch length?

148 How do I decrease the crotch length?

149 I have a large tummy; how can I adjust the pattern here?

150 How can I increase the waistline?

151 How do I take the pattern in at the waist?

152 What do I do if the waistband fits but is gaping at the center back?

153 How do I get the fit around the bottom right?

154 How can I adjust the pattern to fit properly over my hips?

155 One hip is higher than the other; how do I deal with that?

156 My legs curve out slightly; how can I compensate for this?

157 My legs bend in at the knee; how do I alter the pattern?

158 I have a swayback; how can I adjust for this?

159 How do I lengthen pant legs?

160 How do I shorten pant legs?

161 How can I widen the pant legs at the thigh?

162 I have thin thighs; how do I make the pant legs narrower?

163 I want to alter the style of my pant legs; how do I do it?

164 How do I put pleats in pants?

165 How do I take out pleats in pants?

166 The side seam on the pants swings backward; how do I alter the pattern?

167 The pant leg seems to be twisting; what's the problem?

168 How do I know where to put the crease lines?

169 How do I alter the pattern for a flat bottom?

170 How do I know where the knee line is on the pattern?

171 How much hem allowance should I have?

8

ADJUSTING PANTS

Question 145:
How can I tell if the pants will fit?

When you try on pants it's immediately obvious if they don't fit. However, it's not always so easy to tell where they need to be altered. When it comes to the fit of pants, there are a few important factors to consider, but getting the correct measurements for certain body areas will help.

For a good-fitting waist that's tailored and comfortable, you should be able to easily slide two fingers between you and the waistband.

Fabric should glide over the hips with no wrinkles forming at the side seam on the thighs. For dress pants, unlike jeans, a slightly looser fit is more flattering than a snug fit.

The crotch length—also known as the rise—is an important measurement to consider. If it's too short, the pants will be uncomfortable, especially when you sit down. If the crotch length is too long, you will look short in the leg and long in the waist; a good tailored fit for pants does not cling to the crotch.

Pant legs should fall back into place when you stand up and not stay half way up your leg.

For successful pants, choosing the right fabric helps. Substantial materials with a good drape, such as gaberdine, crepe, twill, and linen, are good fabrics for first attempts.

Question 146:
What is the crotch length and how do I measure it?

The crotch length, or rise, is the measurement from your waist at the center front through the legs to the waist on the center back.

To measure the rise or crotch length, hold the tape measure at the center back of your waist (you may need some help taking this measurement). Run the tape between your legs, pulling comfortably at the crotch and up to your natural waist at the center front. How tightly you measure this length will determine whether you need to add ease; usually 1 inch (2.5 cm). Divide the total length in two so that the back crotch measurement is 2 inches (5 cm) longer than the front measurement. Compare the two lengths to your front and back pant patterns, by measuring from the waist to the intersection of the crotch and the inner leg seam.

Front and back crotch measurements differ enormously on larger women. The length can be anything up to 4¾ inches (12 cm) longer in the back than the front, due to a big bottom or full, high hips.

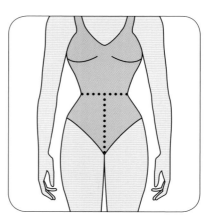

ABOVE To measure the crotch length, tie a string around your waist to get the natural waistline (see Question 51) and then measure from this down between the legs and back up to the string at your back.

Question 147:
How do I increase the crotch length?

You can increase the crotch length at the "lengthening and shortening" line on the pant front and back pieces. Cut along these lines and then spread apart the two pieces of the pattern by the amount required. Add paper to extend the pattern. You will have increased both the front and back crotches but you will also have increased the side seams.

If you only want to lengthen the crotch length on either the front or back, lay out the pattern piece you want to alter and cut along the "lengthening and shortening" line. Spread out the pattern at the crotch area by the required amount and taper to nothing at the side seam. Insert some paper and redraw the cutting lines.

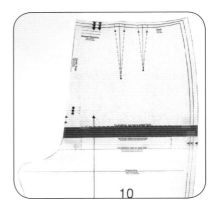

ABOVE Insert paper at the "lengthening" line to increase the crotch length.

Question 148:
How do I decrease the crotch length?

The easiest way to decrease the crotch length is to shorten the pant front and back pieces at the "lengthening and shortening" line. Cut along these lines and then overlap the two pieces of the pattern by the amount required. You will have reduced the crotch in both front and back patterns but be aware you have also decreased the side seams.

If you feel that you only want to shorten the crotch length in either the back or front pattern, lay out the pattern piece you want to alter and cut along the "lengthening and shortening" line. Overlap the pattern at the crotch area by the required amount and taper to nothing at the side seam. Redraw the altered line. The other pants pattern will not be affected.

RIGHT Cut across the "shortening" line and overlap the pattern pieces to reduce the crotch length. Redraw the cutting line at the crotch.

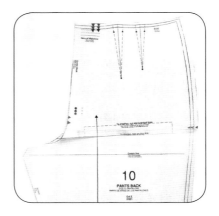

Question 149:

I have a large tummy; how can I adjust the pattern here?

First measure your hip, waist, and fullest part of your tummy. Compare the measurements to your pattern to work out the necessary amounts to be added.

On the front pattern, draw a horizontal line about 3⅛ inches (8 cm) below the waistline from the center front to the side seam. Cut along the line, stopping within ¼ inch (5 mm) of the side seam to leave a "hinge." Draw a line through the center of the waist dart down to the slashed horizontal line. Place paper under the pattern and spread open the horizontal cut to the amount required. Hold this in place while you spread the dart open to

the amount necessary. Tape the altered pattern to the paper and redraw the cutting lines. Trim the paper to the new cutting lines.

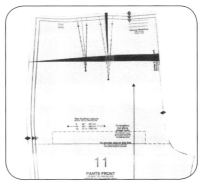

ABOVE To add space for a larger tummy you need to add at the center front.

Question 150:
How can I increase the waistline?

Pants have to have a comfortable waist or they are unbearable to wear. Increasing the waist on pants is a simple pattern alteration so if the rest of the pattern fits well, don't be tempted to use a larger-size pattern.

Measure your waist and the waist on the pattern plus ease and work out the amount you need to add to the pattern. The total should be equally dispersed through the front and back patterns. Throughout the front and back patterns, there are several places that can be adjusted to gain a bit of space: the front and back darts, and the side seams. If you decrease the darts by, say ¼ inch (5 mm), on each side of the dart, you will have gained ½ inch (1 cm) extra with each dart.

To add at the side seams, place paper under the front pattern and draw in a new seam line. The amount you add at the waist will be the amount required divided by four. Taper the new line to the high hip, trying to keep the natural curve of the hip or the pants will appear shapeless. Repeat on the back pattern.

Once you have altered the waistline on the pants, you will need to add the same amount to the waistband. Depending on the style of the waistband, if it's an unshaped pattern, you can add the new amount at one end, but when you have done this, match the waistline with the waistband and realign the notches.

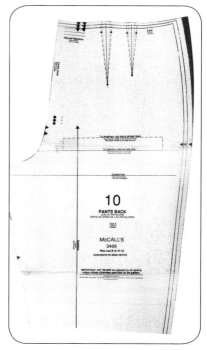

ABOVE If you need to add a lot at the waist, you can both increase at the side seam and decrease the size of the darts.

Question 151:
How do I take the pattern in at the waist?

If you need to reduce the pattern at the waist, it's a simple adjustment.

Measure your waist and the waist on the pattern plus ease and work out the amount you need to take off the pattern. The total should be equally dispersed through the front and back patterns.

If the amount you want to take off the waist is less than about 2 inches (5 cm) in total, then you can easily reduce from the waist at the side seams on both the front and back. Divide the amount by four to work out how much to deduct from each seam. Lay out the front pattern and draw in a new cutting line at the side seam, tapering to nothing above the hip. Repeat with the back pattern piece.

If you need to reduce by more than 2 inches (5 cm) then reduce the side seams and increase the size of all the darts.

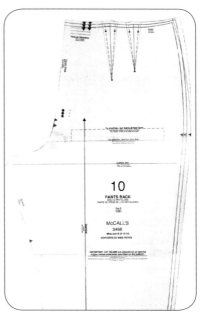

ABOVE Trimming the pattern at the side seam and increasing the size of the darts will enable you take quite a bit off the waist of the pants.

Question 152:
What do I do if the waistband fits but is gaping at the center back?

If you have a slight swayback, you might find that the waistband of your pants is comfortable and fits but there's a gap at the center back.

If the pants fit well, then the waistband is the only part of the pattern to need altering. Lay out the waistband pattern and see whether the pattern is cut in two pieces or made from one piece folded over lengthways. The alteration means shaping the waistband slightly so it will have to be cut in two pieces. Find the point on the waistband pattern where the center back seam would join the waistband. This may be marked with notches or a center fold. Draw two vertical lines, one on either side of the center back, a couple of inches from this point. Fold the pattern at these marked lines and overlap by the required amount, tapering to nothing at the waist edge of the waistband. The amount is dispersed between these two lines and not taken out of the center back so that the waistband stays on the grain line.

When you have completed the alteration, redraw the cutting lines and make sure you have seam allowances all the way around the new waistband. Mark the pattern with "cut two pieces of fabric" to make sure you remember how many pieces to cut!

Question 153:
How do I get the fit around the bottom right?

Wearing pants seems to highlight areas on your body that wouldn't necessarily be noticed when wearing a dress or a skirt. If pants are tight across the bottom, they feel uncomfortable and have an irritating habit of distorting your underwear when moving around.

Lay out the back pant pattern and, depending on how much you need to add, there is a combination of alterations you can make. Start by extending to the back inner leg at the crotch seam adding up to about ¾ inch (2 cm) and tapering to nothing down the inner leg. Don't add more than this as you will end up with too much fabric under the bottom. If you need more room, draw a horizontal line from the side seam to the center back. Cut along the line, stopping within ¼ inch (5 mm) of the side seam to leave a "hinge." Spread open at the center back to the required amount and add extra paper to support the alteration.You can also disperse the fullness over the back pattern, by using one or two darts, as well as altering the length and width, to give the fit you require.

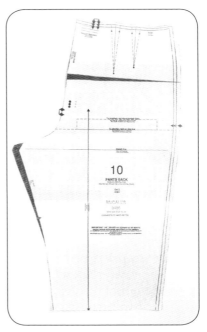

ABOVE Adding to the inner leg on the back pattern and to the back crotch length can help improve the fit around the bottom.

Question 154:
How can I adjust the pattern to fit properly over my hips?

With pants, a slightly looser fit is more flattering than having the fabric straining at the hips, especially on a dress pair. Knowing how to alter the pattern to fit can help. Measure your hips at the widest part and then measure the pattern plus ease, and work out the amount you need to add to the pattern.

Lay out your front pattern and tape some paper under the side seam. Start from nothing on the side seam at the waist, draw a curved line to the point where you want to extend the hip, then with a smooth line taper down above the knee; the exact finishing point will depend on the style of your pant leg. If you need to add a large amount, you will need to add at the side seam too, so start your new seam line a short distance from the waist. Follow the same procedure for the back pattern and when completed, lay the front and back patterns together and check that the side seams and notches match.

RIGHT To add a large amount over the hips you will also have to increase at the waist if you want to get a neat finish.

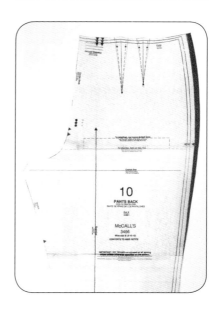

Question 155:
One hip is higher than the other; how do I deal with that?

Most people have one side of their body higher or lower than the other, and hips and shoulders are the most common areas for this to happen.

On pants, if you have one hip higher than the other, you will find diagonal wrinkles appearing near the hip, on the front and back. Make a photocopy of both front and back pant pattern pieces, as you will need to adjust one front and one back piece but still keep the unaltered originals. Lay out the front pattern and draw a horizontal line across the pattern about 1 inch (2.5 cm) below the waist from the center front to the side seam. Cut along the line, stopping within ¼

inch (5 mm) of the center front to leave a "hinge." Place paper underneath and spread open the top piece of pattern to the amount you require. Tape the alteration to the paper. Redraw cutting lines and trim the paper. Alter the back pant pattern in the same way and remember to label the pieces with the side of your body you are adjusting for: left front and left back, or right front and right back. Then when you are ready to cut out the pants use your original pattern to cut out one front and one back piece of fabric, and use your new pattern to cut out the remaining front and back pieces.

Question 156:
My legs curve out slightly; how can I compensate for this?

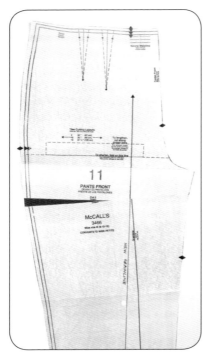 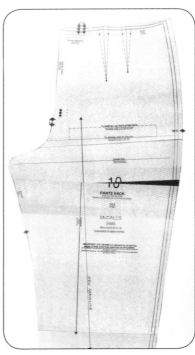

ABOVE To compensate for legs that curve out slightly you need to add to the outside seam and reduce the length of the inner leg seam.

If you discover when you are fitting pants that you have diagonal wrinkles on the side seams which point from the crotch area to the knee, you will have legs that curve out slightly. Therefore you will need to alter the pattern to gain length on the side seams and reduce on the inner leg seams.

Lay out the front pant pattern and draw a horizontal line 1¼–2 inches (3–5 cm) below the crotch point. Cut the pattern across this line. Place paper underneath and overlap the pattern on the inner leg seam below the crotch by about ⅝ inch (1.5 cm). This will automatically spread the pattern open on the side seam by the same amount. Tape the pattern to the paper and at the overlap, and redraw the cutting line; trim the extra paper to this line. Follow the same alteration for the back pant pattern. Redraw the grain line, using the original line below the pattern alteration or the crotch as a guide.

Question 157:

My legs bend in at the knee; how do I alter the pattern?

The pattern alteration for legs that bend in at the knee is the reverse to the adjustments needed for legs that curve out (see Question 156). You need to lengthen the inner leg seams and shorten the side seams.

Lay out the front pant pattern and draw a horizontal line 1¼–2 inches (3–5 cm) below the crotch point. Cut the pattern across this line. Place paper underneath and overlap the pattern on the outer leg seam below the crotch by about ⅝ inch (1.5 cm). This will automatically spread the pattern open on the inner leg seam by the same amount. Tape the pattern to the paper and at the overlap, and redraw the cutting line; trim the extra paper to this line. Follow the same alteration for the back pant pattern. Redraw the grain line, using the original line below the pattern alteration or the crotch as a guide.

Question 158:
I have a swayback; how can I adjust for this?

If you have a swayback, you might find horizontal folds or wrinkles appearing in the small of your back. Altering a pair of pants if you have a swayback, uses the same pattern adaptation as a skirt (see Question 119).

Lay out the back pant pattern and draw a horizontal line from the center back to the side seam 2–3¼ inches (5–8 cm) below the waistline. Cut along the line, stopping within ¼ inch (5 mm) of the side seam to leave a "hinge." Overlap the pattern by the required amount. Redraw the center back cutting line and the darts if they have been affected.

This alteration reduces the back waistline and this is usually necessary if you have a swayback. If, however, you need the normal waistline width, add the amount deducted from the center back to the side seam, tapering to nothing at the hipline.

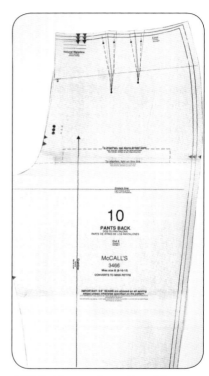

ABOVE After you have altered the center back seam, remember to reposition the darts at the waist.

Question 159:
How do I lengthen pant legs?

To lengthen pants by small amounts—1¼–2 inches (3–5 cm)—you can increase the length at the hem. However, if you have a larger amount to add, you should disperse the amount between two points over the pant leg. You need to lengthen both above and below the knee. By adding at two positions, you keep the proportion of the pant leg.

Find the "lengthening and shortening" line on the pant leg. Cut through this line and place some paper underneath the pattern. Open out the pattern to your required amount and then tape to the paper. Remember to add the same amount to both front and back pant patterns.

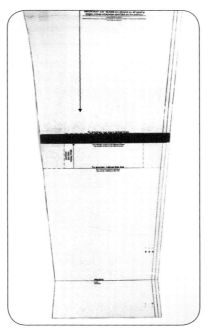

ABOVE Cut across the pant leg at the "lengthen here" line to separate the pattern in two and add in a new section of paper.

Question 160:
How do I shorten pant legs?

To shorten pants by small amounts—1¼–2 inches (3–5 cm)—you can lose some of the length at the hem, but if you have a larger measurement, you should disperse this between two points over the pant leg above the knee and below the knee. This helps you keep the proportion of the pant leg.

Find the "lengthening and shortening" line on the pattern and fold up the pattern along the line to take out the required amount. Tape the alteration in place. Remember to reduce the front and back pant patterns by the same amount. When shortening the pattern you will find that you need to redraw the cutting lines at the side seams. Trim the pattern to these new lines.

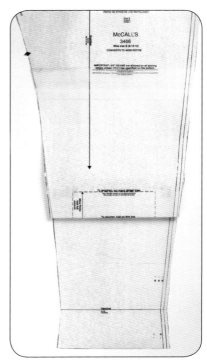

ABOVE Shortening a pant leg is a simple matter of folding the pattern by the required amount at the "shorten here" line.

Question 161:
How can I widen the pant legs at the thigh?

The areas on the pattern where you might consider widening the pant legs will depend on where you want the extra room.

If you need a little more room in the thigh area, lay out your front pant patterns and tape some paper to the inside leg seam. Draw in a new seam line, adding up to 1½ inches (4 cm), and extending from the crotch point and tapering to nothing just below the knee. Repeat with the back pant pattern piece. It's not necessary to add anything to the side seams and in fact doing this will not help eliminate tightness in the thigh area. Check that all the seams and notches match.

Thigh muscles can bulge at the front of even the slimmest legs and the pattern may need a little tweaking to accommodate this. Follow the same alteration as above but only add to the front inside leg seam; don't alter the back pattern piece. Check that all seams and notches match.

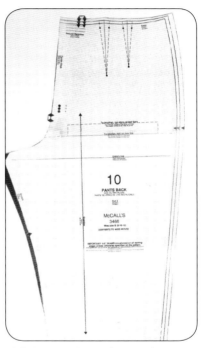

ABOVE Increasing at the inner leg, between crotch and knee, can give you more room in the thigh.

Question 162:
I have thin thighs; how do I make the pant legs narrower?

If you have slim thighs, you may want to alter the pant pattern to take out any bagginess in this area.

Lay out your front pant patterns. Draw in a new seam line on the inside leg, reducing by up to 1½ inches (4 cm). Extend the new line from the crotch point and taper to nothing just below the knee. Draw in a new cutting line at the crotch point. Trim the altered pattern to the new cutting line. Repeat with the back pant pattern piece.

It's not necessary to take anything off at the side seams since this will not reduce the area over the thigh. Check that all the seams and notches match.

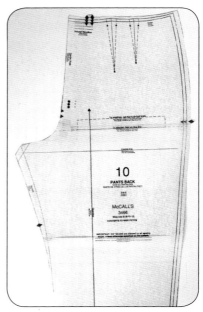

ABOVE If you reduce the pant width at the inner leg, this will reduce any bagginess in the thighs.

Question 163:
I want to alter the style of my pant legs; how do I do it?

Once you have the fit you are happy with for your pants, you may want to change the style of the leg width according to the fashion of the moment, such as straight cut, flared, or tapered.

Lay out your front and back pant patterns and if you want to taper or widen the leg by a small amount—1¼–2 inches (3–5 cm) in total—you can add or take this off the outer side seams only. For greater amounts, add or subtract on each seam. Decide on the total amount and divide by four. To taper, draw in a new seam line the required amount from the hem, tapering to nothing at about knee level. To add a flare, tape paper to both side seams on both front and back pattern pieces and draw in new seams, tapering to nothing at about knee level.

ABOVE There's a variety of different pant leg styles from which to choose.

Question 164:
How do I put pleats in pants?

Pleats are a great styling detail to add to pants made from a fabric that drapes well, such as crepe or linen.

If you want fullness all the way to the hem, then your pleat needs to extend the full length of the pant leg. Lay out the front pant pattern and draw a vertical line from the center of the waist to the center of the hem. Follow the grain line and if the pattern has darts, you can include them into the pleat width. Cut along the line, stopping within ¼ inch (5 mm) of the hem to leave a "hinge." Put paper under the pattern—you may have to tape several sheets of paper together to get the right length. Spread the pattern at the waist to the desired amount, tapering to nothing at the hem. Straighten the cutting line at the hem.

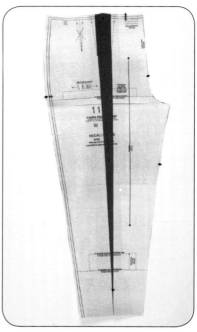

ABOVE You can add a pleat through the whole length of the pant leg.

EXPERT TIP

66 **When altering pant patterns, the grain line can sometimes distort. A quick way of checking that the front pant pattern has the correct grain is to draw a horizontal line from the front crotch to the side seam, measure the distance, and then mark the halfway point. Then draw a vertical line perpendicular to the horizontal line and the hem; this is your new grain line. 99**

If you want the leg to maintain the same width at the knee and below, draw a horizontal line from the side seam to the vertical line you have drawn from the waist. Cut the vertical line down to where it meets the horizontal line, then cut along the horizontal toward the side seam, stopping within ¼ inch (5 mm) of the side seam to leave a "hinge." Spread the pattern at the waist and you will be left with a dip on the side seam near the hinge. Redraw and smooth the side seams.

Question 165:

How do I take out pleats in pants?

Lay out your front pant pattern and measure the waist, excluding the pleats. When removing pleats you have to consider that the pants still need to have shape at the waist in the form of one or two front darts. Draw a vertical line through the center of the pleat at the waist to the hem. Cut along the line, stopping within ¼ inch (5 mm) of the hem to leave a "hinge." Close the pleat by overlapping the pattern at the waist making sure you leave at least 1¼ inches (3 cm) for each dart at the waist. Redraw the front darts starting at the waist and tapering to a point at about 3¼ inches (8 cm) from the waist. If the original darts are not in the right place, they can be repositioned depending on where you need them.

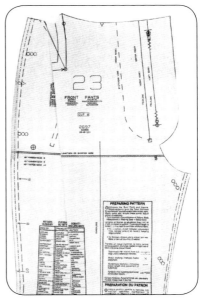

ABOVE When you've cut and overlapped the pattern to take out the pleat, redraw the pleat (or pleats).

Question 166:
The side seam on the pants swings backward; how do I alter the pattern?

There are several reasons why the side seam on a pair of pants might be swinging backward and before altering the pattern, it's worth checking a couple of areas on the pattern.

The grain line is the first area to look at. Start by confirming that the pattern has been cut on the straight grain of the fabric. Care must be taken when laying out the fabric and pinning pattern pieces to the fabric; check that each piece is placed parallel with the selvedge (see Question 76) before cutting. If the pattern is not positioned on the grain, the fabric will not hang correctly when the garment is constructed.

If the grain line is correct, you need to reduce the side seam of the front pattern piece and increase the side seam on the back pattern piece in order to get the side seam into the right position. Decide on how much you need to add to the front piece and lay out the front pattern flat. Take off the required amount on the side seam, starting at the hem tapering to nothing at the hipline. Trim to the new cutting line.

Lay out the back pattern piece and tape paper to the side seam between the hip and hem—you may need to tape sheets of paper together to get enough. Draw in the new seam line, adding the same amount you reduced on the front pattern, tapering to nothing at the same point on the hip. Redraw any cutting lines and trim to the cutting lines. Place both front and back side patterns together to check that the notches match.

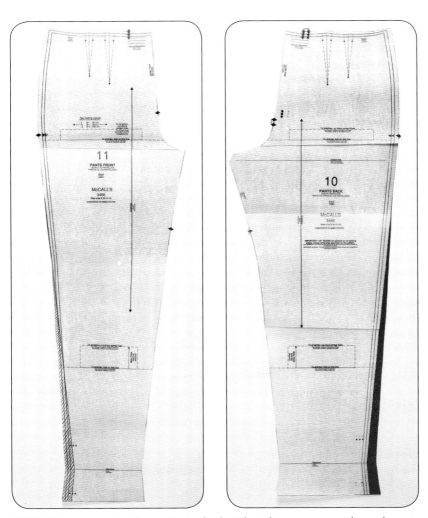

ABOVE To stop pant legs from swinging back at the side seam, you need to reduce at the side seam on the front piece and add to the side seam on the back piece.

Question 167:
The pant leg seems to be twisting; what's the problem?

The main reason pants tend to twist is that the pattern has not been cut on the straight grain of the fabric. Take care to check that each pattern piece is placed parallel with the selvedge (see Question 76).

If you cut the fabric on the grain correctly and your pants are still twisting, then the grain line position on the pattern needs to be checked. The Expert Tip in Question 164 covers checking the grain line on the front piece. To check it on the back pattern, draw a horizontal line from the crotch point to the side seam. Find the halfway point on this line and mark a point 1 inch (2.5 cm) in toward the side seam. Draw a vertical line through the marked spot and perpendicular to the hem and the new horizontal line; this is your new grain line.

Question 168:
How do I know where to put the crease lines?

Crease lines on pants give a professional finish, especially if they have pleats. If you decide to put creases into your pants, it's easier to achieve if they are pressed into the fabric before the pants are completely sewn together.

To find the crease-line position, line up the inner and outer legs with the seams together from the knee to the hem. From the knee upward, let the pattern stay on the grain line. When pressing the crease lines on a flat-fronted pair of pants, the crease usually finishes at the crotch seam area on both the front and back, while making sure they are the same height front and back.

On pleated pants, the front crease and pleat is pressed all the way to the waist; the back crease is only pressed to the crotch seam.

Question 169:
How do I alter the pattern for a flat bottom?

One of the signs of having a flat bottom or seat is that when you are wearing pants, wrinkles are obvious under or near the bottom. This is because there is too much length and width across the bottom area.

Lay out the back pant pattern and draw a horizontal line about 4 inches (10 cm) below the waist from the side seam to the center back. Cut along the line, stopping within ¼ inch (5 mm) of the side seam to leave a "hinge." Overlap the pattern to reduce by the necessary amount and then redraw the center back line. You may also find the dart is

quite full and sticks out, especially if you only have one dart, so you can either distribute into two darts or decrease by the extra amount by taking out on the waistline at the side seam, then smooth the curve into the hipline. For a flat bottom, having two darts rather than one can help with achieving a smoother fit; make the dart nearer the center back 1¼–1½ inches (3–4 cm) longer than the dart nearer the side seam. You can also decrease the inside back leg seam at the crotch, tapering to nothing. Remember to check that the back and front inside seams match after altering.

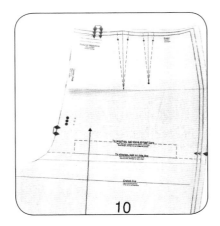

RIGHT Cut across the back pattern piece and then overlap at the center back seam to reduce in the bottom area.

Question 170:
How do I know where the knee line is on the pattern?

It's useful to know where the knee line is on a pants pattern if you need to alter it in any way. When tapering or increasing the width of the pant leg you need to adjust to the knee point.

Lay out your front pattern piece and mark the fullest part of the hip with a horizontal line from the crotch to the side seam, then fold up the hem allowance on the pant leg. Fold the pant leg so the hem crease touches the marked hipline. The newly formed crease in the pant leg is the knee line.

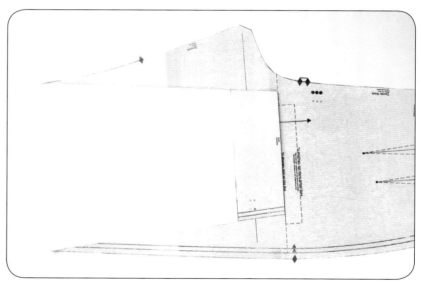

ABOVE By folding the pant leg in the correct way, you can easily find the position of the knee.

Question 171:
How much hem allowance should I have?

The hem on a pair of pants is more than just the finish for the raw edge of the fabric at the end of the pant legs. It also maintains the shape of the garment. A well-made pair of pants should have a hem of about 1½–2 inches (4–5 cm) in depth. This gives the fabric of the legs enough weight and substance to hang well on the body.

To produce a clean, crisp, pressed hem, it helps to fuse a strip of interfacing on the wrong side of the fabric on the hem areas on both the front and back pieces. Use your pattern pieces as a guide to cut out the correct-sized piece of interfacing. Press the interfacing in place after you've cut out the garment pieces and before you sew them together.

With the fused hem you will find pressing easier, especially in fabrics such as linen, cotton, and crepe. Only press the hem edge and never where you have stitched the hem to the pant leg as the iron often leaves an impression of the stitching underneath.

172 What is a basic block?

173 What is the difference between a block and a sloper?

174 Can I buy a commercial block pattern?

175 If I construct a block pattern, how should it fit?

176 What is balance in a garment?

177 How do I stop the patterns from becoming a mess?

178 Is the lining pattern the same as the garment pattern?

179 I would like princess seams instead of darts; how do I do this?

180 How do you get flare on a straight skirt with darts?

181 How can I join a bodice and skirt together to make a dress pattern?

182 How do I reproduce a favorite pair of pants?

183 How do I make a false hem for a skirt?

184 The commercial pattern I have seems to have separate facings; can I join them?

185 How do I make a facing?

9

FURTHER WAYS TO CREATE AND ADAPT PATTERNS

Question 172:
What is a basic block?

A basic block is the master pattern drafted to a set of body measurements plus ease. The block has no styling within the pattern, just basic darts, and it fits the body snugly without any design ease; a garment made up from the block without any styling can be unforgiving when you wear it. The block is used as a starting point or marker to make other patterns of a similar style, with design or styling and ease added to the fashion pattern and not the original basic block. The basic master block cannot be used with other patterns by tracing off parts of the block, such as the armhole, as it doesn't contain the correct ease for an everyday garment and won't work.

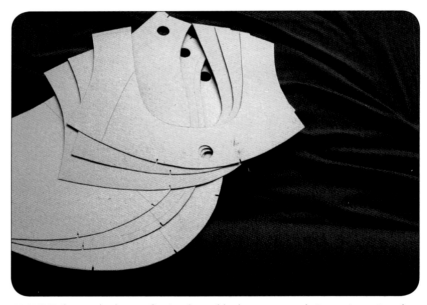

ABOVE Tailors and other professionals use block patterns as their starting point when constructing garments.

Further Ways to Create and Adapt Patterns

Question 173:
What is the difference between a block and a sloper?

The strictest definition of the word "sloper" is that it's any pattern without seam allowances, or "net." The term is not used solely by the clothing industry, it's also used by any manufacturer who is producing something made from fabric—from a car seat to a couch cover. There is slight confusion over the word but generally most people use the word "sloper" to refer to a basic fitting shell made up from a set of measurements, either to an industry standard or to personal ones.

In the fashion industry the word "block" is always used and never the term "sloper" but we can safely assume that it's the same thing.

Question 174:
Can I buy a commercial block pattern?

Most pattern companies sell block patterns or fitting shells, with each company developing a slightly different pattern depending on the measurements they use. The block is the master pattern for every garment designed by that particular pattern manufacturer.

If you like the designs produced by a particular pattern company, it's worth making up the block pattern or fitting shell produced by that company so you know what to expect when making their various garments. Pattern companies not only differ in the measurements they use but also in the amount of ease they allow, as well as in the shoulder length, bust shaping, and armhole depth.

Question 175:
If I construct a block pattern, how should it fit?

The advantages of making and fitting a block pattern is that once you have it fitting perfectly, you will know where your body differs to the block and will then be able to make pattern adjustments accordingly, such as the bust area. You should make a toile out of calico (or other suitable fabric) to assess the fit of the block (see Questions 58 to 61).

A basic block generally fits where it touches the body, so when you try on the toile it can feel uncomfortable when bending your elbows in the sleeves, as the design or styling ease is not added to the block. However, the armhole should not feel restricted and you should have movement around the arms. Check that the seams and darts are in the correct places and that the side seams are not swaying forward or backward.

There are usually two darts on the front bodice and one dart on the back bodice; these are then manipulated into other positions on your fashion pattern depending on the design.

EXPERT TIP

66 A good firm fabric such as calico or cotton gingham is suitable for making up a toile from the basic block. Gingham can be useful as the lines and squares act like a grid and will move out of place, making it easier to identify fitting problems. 99

Question 176:
What is balance in a garment?

Posture is generally determined by the way a person stands. Variations in posture can affect the balance of a garment.

The correct balance of a garment is where the hemline is parallel to the ground and the center back, and center front lines and side seams are perpendicular to the ground.

Many factors affect the balance of a garment and most pattern alterations for specific problem areas have been covered so far, but there are a few other areas to look at when checking for general balance. Firstly, check for short back length caused by a slightly stooping posture; this can be diagnosed if the garment is pulling at the upper back. If you have very straight posture and the garment pulls at the front, the front length is short. If diagonal folds appear from the back waist running to the bust and result in the front of the garment hanging away from the body at the center front, then the back and side lengths are too long.

RIGHT If you draw a line on the center front of the toile, you will easily see any discrepancies caused by, say, one shoulder being higher than the other.

EXPERT TIP

66 **When cutting out the block or fitting shell mark the center front, center back, waistline, bust, and hiplines on the fabric with pencil or pen. With the help of these guidelines, you will have an indicator of the balance when trying on the garment.** 99

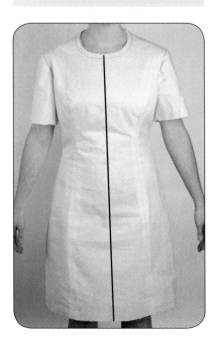

Question 177:
How do I stop the patterns from becoming a mess?

Once you have started to adapt patterns and understand the importance of good-fitting garments, you will want to alter and combine patterns for most projects. A word of caution first; it's incredibly easy to forget what you have altered and get into a mess, especially if you are in a hurry and just want to get something finished. There are a few tips to make pattern management easier.

Attempt to be methodical when altering a pattern by putting aside enough time so you don't have to leave a pattern half altered and assume you will remember what you have and have not adjusted. Get into the habit of writing a note of what you have done to a pattern as well as the date and storing this note with the pattern. Always remember to label altered pattern pieces with the name of the garment part; it's no use finding a blank shape included in the envelope. If you do combine pieces from different patterns, make sure they all go back into their original envelopes when you've finished. When you have completed a task, take time to clear the space carefully before you start another project.

Question 178:
Is the lining pattern the same as the garment pattern?

A lining finishes off seams neatly and makes a garment more opaque as well as easier to put on and take off. The lining is generally cut from the same pattern pieces as the garment for skirts, dresses, and pants. If, however, your design has facings, the lining pattern will be cut differently since it has to attach to the facings. The lining pattern for jackets and coats is cut with more ease around the back and the arms and the pattern allows for the hem and any facings.

Question 179:
I would like princess seams instead of darts; how do I do this?

Princess seams are a styling detail that look good if you require more shaping over the bust. The darts on the front and back bodice are changed into seams, starting mid-shoulder and continue down to the waistline or farther to the hem if you are making a dress.

Lay out your front pattern and decide where you want the seam to start at the shoulder. Draw a line from this through to the bust point. Then continue drawing a line down through the center of the waist dart to the hem. (If there are two darts at the waist, draw through the one nearest the side seam.) Mark two notches on this line above and below the bust point to help with matching the seams. Round off the angle at the bust point with a curved ruler. Cut the pattern in half along this line.

You then need to eliminate the original darts. Cut through the center of the bust dart and (if the pattern has two waist darts) the center of the waist dart nearest the center front. Then overlap the darts and tape down. You now have two pieces: the side front panel and

front panel. Using your new pattern pieces as templates, divide the back pattern piece into two panels to match the front. Make sure the shoulder and side seams still match up. When you cut out your fabric pieces you must remember to add allowances to the new seams you have created.

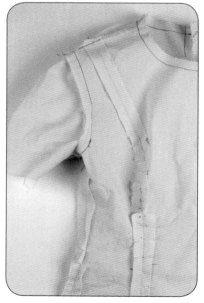

ABOVE A princess seam (seen here on the wrong side of a toile) runs from the shoulder, over the bust, to the hem.

Question 180:
How do you get flare on a straight skirt with darts?

Once you have found a skirt pattern that fits, you may want to modify the style. The amount of flare you want to add to a skirt is personal preference, but it's worth bearing in mind what fabric you are going to use: softer, more fluid fabrics such as silk look better with a generous amount of flare in the pattern.

First, lay out your front skirt pattern and draw two vertical lines from waist to hem, parallel to the center front. Draw one of the lines through the center of the waist dart. The aim is to divide the pattern into three more-or-less equal parts. Cut along the drawn lines, stopping within ¼

inch (5 mm) of the waist to leave a "hinge." Place paper underneath the pattern—you may need to tape sheets together to get a big enough piece. Open up the hem at each cut line to the required amount, trying to keep equal proportions between each slashed part. Add at the side seam if you want; this will close the dart at the waist. Tape the pattern in place. Check the waist measurement and reshape the cutting line as necessary. Repeat the same alteration on the back skirt pattern piece, remembering to add the same amount of flare as you did to the front pattern piece.

Question 181:
How can I join a bodice and skirt together to make a dress pattern?

If you have a bodice pattern which fits well and a skirt pattern that you like, it is fairly straightforward to combine both patterns to make a dress. The bodice pattern could be from a top or blouse, or from a dress: if you use the bodice from a dress, make sure you find and mark the position of the waistline.

Before you start combining patterns, check that the waist measurements and dart styling on the two patterns are similar, as this can reduce the time spent drafting the pattern. The following example is for a bodice with a bust dart and a skirt with a dart.

Lay out a large sheet of paper and place the front bodice pattern on top; trace around it. Then place your front skirt pattern on the paper and match the two waistlines at the center front and the side seam, excluding seam allowances. If the darts on the bodice don't match the skirt, adjust the skirt to match the bodice pattern and don't worry if you have to adjust the size of the darts at the waist. The side seams are also likely to be slightly different but find an average and

redraw the line. Draw around the rest of the skirt piece and cut out the new pattern.

The same method is used to combine the back bodice and skirt pattern. When you have adjusted the pattern, check that all seams and notches match.

ABOVE You can combine the pattern for a puff-sleeved bodice and a long skirt to create a new dress.

Question 182:
How do I reproduce a favorite pair of pants?

If you have a pair of store-bought pants that you love, it's worth hanging onto them and when you are looking for a commercial pattern, try to find a similar style and then set about trying to personlize the pattern.

First, turn your pants inside out and take as many measurements as possible to compare with the commercial pattern. Look at the crotch length and width of the thighs, knee, waist, hip, and hem measurements. Lay out the pattern and measure the same points to compare. You could also place the inside-out pants onto the back curve, comparing the crotch length from the waist to the inner leg seam. The pattern can be altered with the "lengthening and shortening" line as well as other adjustments covered in Chapter 8.

Once you have adjusted the pattern to your measurements, it's worth making a toile to check your pattern alterations.

EXPERT TIP

66 **When measuring a crotch seam on a pair of pants, instead of measuring with the tape measure flat, run the tape around curved seams on it's side, making it accurate and flexible.** 99

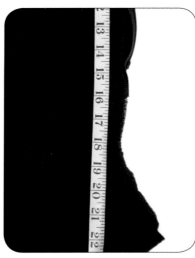

ABOVE Measure the crotch length when assessing the size of an existing pair of pants.

Question 183:
How do I make a false hem for a skirt?

There could be several reasons why you may need a false hem on your skirt. Perhaps you don't have enough fabric or the skirt is too short.

This technique doesn't require a specific pattern and is useful when altering garments. Cut a strip of fabric on the true bias (see Question 71) in the desired width and depth of the hem plus seam allowances. Turn under one long raw edge of the bias strip and machine stitch in place. Pin the bias fabric to the hem edge of the garment, with right sides together and matching the raw edges; try not to stretch the bias as you work your way around the skirt. Turn the bias strip up toward the inside of the skirt and press the new hem edge down. Then handstitch the hem to the skirt. You could also topstitch along the bottom hem edge if you like.

ABOVE Instead of extending the length of a skirt pattern at the hem, you could cut the pattern to the given length and then use a false hem to finish.

Question 184:
The commercial pattern I have seems to have separate facings; can I join them?

Just because a commercial pattern is constructed in a certain way it doesn't mean you can't change it. Facings are a good example of this; they don't always have to be made from a separate piece and on center fronts and straight hems; it may be more convenient to be "grown on."

For example, you might like a grown-on facing on a center front for a blouse or top. Lay out your front pattern and mark the sewing line on the center front; this is usually ⅝ inch (1.5 cm) in from the cutting line. Do the same with the line on the center front of the corresponding facing piece. Trim off or fold under both pattern pieces along this line.

Pin the front pattern onto your fabric. Then place the facing pattern next to it and match the two center fronts together on the sewing line; pin into place. When you cut out the fabric you should have a grown-on facing (see Questions 113 and 114 for grown-on waistbands).

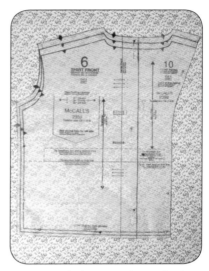

ABOVE Mark the sewing line on both pattern pieces and then trim (or fold under) at this line. Pin the two pattern pieces on the fabric matched at the sewing line.

Question 185:
How do I make a facing?

A facing can be a simple way of finishing off the edge on a garment. Adding facing will mean you don't have to turn under edges and hem them—which can be tricky on curved edges such as armholes and necklines. On a skirt or a pair of pants, you won't have to finish the waist with a waistband.

To make a facing for a skirt, lay out your front and back skirt patterns and place some paper underneath, trace off the top sections of the skirt, around the waist and side seams, and roughly cut out the sections. Darts are not needed on facings, so you can either eliminate them when you are tracing the pattern or draw in the darts and then close and tape them together. Make sure you have a smooth cutting line around the waist and hem of the facings. Remember to include seam allowances and mark notches between the facing and the waist.

HOW IT'S DONE

When you are making a new pattern for a facing you can trace around your existing pattern.

• Place the pattern on your dot-and-cross paper (see Question 6) and draw around the outside—you don't have to draw around the whole pattern, just the area where you want to add the facing.

• Take the pattern off the paper and then draw in a bottom edge for your facing. You need to make sure the facing will be deep enough not to ride up during wear.

• If you have access to a photocopier, then you can simply make a copy of the pattern and then draw in your new facing. Trim the photocopy to create a new pattern.

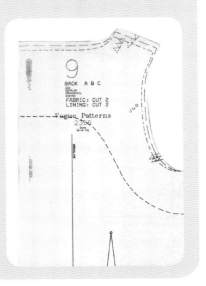

186 How do I make a zipper look good?

187 What sort of seams should I do?

188 How do I make the sleeve head look good?

189 How do I make hems look crisp?

190 How do I stop seams from becoming bulky?

191 How do I sew a lining in without hand sewing?

192 How do I fuse the interlining without distortion?

193 How do I stop armholes and necklines from stretching?

194 What's the secret to achieving perfect buttonholes?

195 Where do I understitch?

196 How do I get a slit or vent to sit correctly at the back of a skirt?

197 What's a mitred corner?

198 How do I attach a shoulder pad?

199 What is "clipping a seam"?

200 How do I sew jersey fabric?

10

ACHIEVING A PROFESSIONAL-LOOKING FINISH

Question 186:
How do I make a zipper look good?

One of the easiest and most effective zippers to use is the invisible or concealed zipper. It's regularly used on dresses, skirts, and pants and gives a professional finish.

When attaching the zipper to the seam, it's worth spending a little time preparing the fabric before sewing. A strip of interfacing, about ¾ inch (2 cm) wide, fused to the wrong side of the fabric on the seam allowance where the zipper is to be inserted, stabilizes the area and stops any fabric movement when using the zipper foot.

To ensure the zipper is inserted correctly, sew up the seam where the zipper is to go with small tacking stitches to about ⅝ inch (1.5 cm) above the anticipated zipper end; lightly press the seam open. Pin and tack the zipper in position on the seam, attaching it to the seam allowance only. Fit your sewing machine with a zipper foot and stitch each side of the zipper to the seam allowance. Stitch as close to the teeth as possible. Check that the zipper is lying flat and not distorting the seam in any way, then undo the tacking stitches. At the bottom of the zipper you will not be able to sew exactly to the point of the seam but about ¼ inch (5 mm) away; this is acceptable and will still give you a good finish.

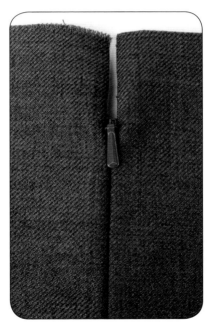

ABOVE Tacking the seam together before inserting a zipper helps keep the zipper concealed after it has been stitched in place.

Question 187:
What sort of seams should I do?

When sewing together a garment, there are many types of seams you can do, such as lapped seams, French seams, and flat-fell seams. The choice may seem daunting but the aim of each seam is the same—to join two pieces of fabric and then neaten the edges to stop fraying.

A plain seam is most commonly used with the raw edges overlocked or serged; this gives a fast as well as a neat finish but you will need a purpose-made machine (see Question 11). If you don't have an overlocker, you can finish seam edges with a zigzag stitch; this is usually found as a separate setting on your sewing machine.

A French seam encloses all raw edges and involves sewing two seams. This method makes any additional finishing unnecessary and produces a strong seam. It's often used on sheer or delicate fabrics, and is good for childrenswear as there are no raw edges exposed. The seam looks like a plain seam from the front but on the reverse it resembles a tuck. Place the wrong sides of the fabric together and stitch a seam, taking a ¼ inch (5 mm) allowance. Press the seam to one side. Fold the fabric so the right sides are together. Stitch another seam, taking a ⅜ inch (1 cm) allowance, to enclose the first seam.

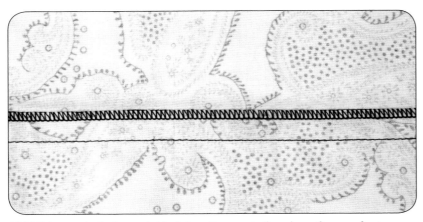

ABOVE An overlocked seam is ideal since it prevents the edges of a seam fraying.

Question 188:
How do I make the sleeve head look good?

A smoothly fitted sleeve is one of the signs of a professional-looking garment. The set-in sleeve is cut with the sleeve cap having more fullness than the armhole section and yet it's designed to fit. It requires skill to distribute the ease evenly over the sleeve head. Sleeves that are less problematic are the shirt sleeve, dolman sleeve, and the raglan sleeve, which are variations of the set-in sleeve but fit into a deeper or irregularly shaped armhole.

After you have cut your sleeve pieces out of the fabric, tack or machine baste around the sleeve head between the notches, leaving long threads at either end of the stitching. Stitch together your sleeve at the seams. When you come to attach the sleeves to your bodice, pull the threads at either end of the tacking to gather the fabric over the sleeve head until it fits into the armhole. Insert the sleeve into the armhole and pin and tack in place. Check that the fit is alright before machine stitching.

ABOVE Use tacking stitches to gather up the sleeve head to fit the armhole.

EXPERT TIP

❝ Sometimes, even with a shoulder pad, the ease on the sleeve head can look puffy. Inside top-quality tailored jackets and wool dresses you will find a sleeve-head roll; this enables the sleeve to "roll over" the shoulder end by padding and filling the ease. To imitate this, cut a strip of spongy interlining or padding about 1¼ inches (3 cm) wide and stitch into the top third of the armhole following the previous row of stitching. ❞

Question 189:
How do I make hems look crisp?

The hem is usually the final step in completing your sewing project and an indicator of the quality of the garment. A decent hem maintains the shape and body of the style.

Your chosen hem finish will depend on the garment style and fabric weight. Don't be afraid to examine hem types when out clothes shopping and becoming aware, for example, that a chiffon fabric will have a small pin hem rather than a 1½ inches (4 cm) turning, or that a gored skirt may have a small overlocked and turned hem, with an expensive version possibly having a hem facing.

HOW IT'S DONE

To make hems and hem facings look crisp, you need to use interfacing.
• Cut a strip of interfacing to cover the depth of hem allowance for each pattern piece—use the pattern pieces as a guide to the length of the strip.
• Fuse the interfacing to the wrong side of the fabric. For lightweight fabrics make sure you can't see the interfacing on the right side of the fabric.
• Once fused, continue to hem as normal and press the edge of the hem only.

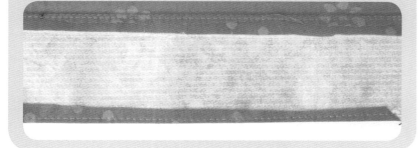

Question 190:
How do I stop seams from becoming bulky?

If you are using thick fabrics such as wool suiting or denim, you may find you have bulky seams that don't press flat and look unattractive. This can also happen at points where two or three seams meet, such as on collars or cuffs.

First you need to grade or layer the seam allowance, which means cutting the allowance within the seam to different lengths. Trim any facings and interfacings close to the sewing line and then trim down each layer of fabric in the seam. This eliminates a ridge being formed by the bulk of several layers of fabric and stops a shadow line from forming on the right side when pressed. When working with thick wool fabrics you may find you are left with a bulky seam even after grading. A pressing tool called a clapper board can be used to flatten the seam or bulky area by steaming the area on the garment, keeping it hot, and then clapping it with the board. Always use a press cloth and test all fabrics first.

ABOVE To grade a seam, trim each layer of fabric so that it is shorter than the one underneath. Don't trim too close to the stitching though.

Achieving a Professional-Looking Finish

Question 191:
How do I sew a lining in without hand sewing?

Lining a garment gives a professional finish and always looks impressive. It may appear to be difficult but if approached in a methodical manner it's no more difficult than constructing the main garment. In effect, all you are doing is linking together two "shells."

If you are making a lined jacket, you should first construct the main garment—the outer "shell." Then stitch together the lining—the inner "shell"—in exactly the same way but leave an opening of at least 6 inches (15 cm) on one underarm sleeve seam. This is where you turn the garment right side out.

Pin the garment and the lining right sides together, matching the center back, shoulders, notches, and sleeve hems. Machine stitch all the way around the front edges to about 2 inches (5 cm) from the hem. Then machine stitch the sleeve lining to the sleeve hem.

Pin the garment hem and machine stitch from one side to another leaving a gap of about 6 inches (15 cm) somewhere in the middle of the hem. Turn the jacket to the right side and check that the lining is hanging correctly.

At this point you may want to loosely attach the underarm lining to the underarm seam allowance of the garment. Find the gap in the sleeve and pull through the unclosed hem area and machine stitch together. Finally you are only left with a gap in the sleeve seam that can be pinned and machine stitched together.

Question 192:
How do I fuse the interlining without distortion?

Commercial patterns suggest using the relevant pattern pieces to cut out the interfacing you need for sections such as collars and cuffs. Having cut out and fused the small parts as directed you may find that, after making up the garment, perhaps the undercollar is twisting or that one cuff sits better than the other. This is because the pattern pieces have been distorted during the fusing process before any sewing has taken place making it impossible to rectify. The solution is a process that is known in the fashion industry as block fusing.

HOW IT'S DONE

Block fuse smaller pattern pieces in the following way.
• First cut out bits of fabric that are roughly big enough for your small pattern pieces.
• Cut out bits of interfacing roughly the same size.
• Fuse the fabric and interfacing together.
• Position the pattern pieces on top, pin, and cut out.

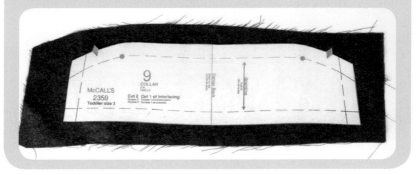

Question 193:
How do I stop armholes and necklines from stretching?

Once you have pinned the pattern to the fabric and cut it out, you are probably anxious to get started on your sewing project. However, it's worth taking a little time to prepare the cut-out fabric pieces, because stretching and distortion of armholes and necklines starts happening the moment you begin to handle the fabric. This is because many of these areas are often angled or curved, and are, therefore, actually cut on the bias.

Most commercial patterns refer to stay-stitching around necklines. This means simply machine stitching a line of stitching around the neckline in a place that won't be seen on the right side. This is an acceptable method of stabilizing the fabric, but if you are working with a "difficult" fabric and want to be more precise, then you can use interfacing. Cut a strip of interfacing about ¾ inch (2 cm) wide to overlap the seam allowance. Cut to the length or shape of the armhole—snip into it to shape roughly around curves. Fuse in place.

ABOVE A strip of interfacing, cut to fit, will stabilize a neckline on a lightweight fabric and help you to achieve a clean finish when the garment is constructed.

Question 194:
What's the secret to achieving perfect buttonholes?

Buttonholes are usually the last step before your garment is finished and can "make" or "break" an item of clothing. A well-made shirt can be let down by badly sewn buttonholes.

Most sewing machines have a buttonhole foot and once you have checked with the manual, it's relatively simple to set the correct length for your chosen button. It's vital to test the buttonhole on a scrap of fabric first, as well as checking the buttonhole placement. It's very easy to make a mistake, but very time consuming to unpick a buttonhole and virtually impossible to remove the markings the thread makes on the fabric if you are wrong. And, of course, if you cut through the fabric at the buttonhole before realizing your mistake, you are stuck with the problem.

Always use interfacing and fuse the area where the buttonholes will go on the facing and the center front or cuff. The fusing stabilizes the fabric and prevents the tight stitching of a buttonhole from bunching up the fabric.

Never use a seam ripper to cut open buttonholes, as they are designed for ripping open seams, not careful cutting. Seam rippers can also distort the buttonholes on loosely woven or delicate fabrics.

Question 195:
Where do I understitch?

Understitching is a sewing technique used to keep garment linings and facings from rolling out and being visible. It's a quick method that helps give a finished look to clothing and ensures a better fit on the body.

Understitching is used on arm, neck, or hem facings, as well as skirts and pants that use facings rather than a waistband.

After sewing a seam and having trimmed or overlocked, press the seam carefully toward the facing, making sure that you are precise and there are no folds. On the right side of the garment facing, use a straight stitch about ¼ inch (5 mm) from the sewing line and close enough to capture the seam allowance. Turn the facing to the inside of the garment and press again.

Always attach facings in strategic points to the garment; for example, underarm seams or shoulder seams, as this prevents the facings from rolling out and being seen.

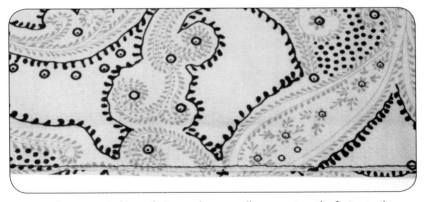

ABOVE After stay-stitching a facing to the seam allowance, turn the facing to the inside of the garment and press again. The stitching will be visible on the wrong side of the garment only.

Question 196:

How do I get a slit or vent to sit correctly at the back of a skirt?

If you have ever made a skirt with a vent or split at the center back, you may well have experienced problems with the hang of the skirt at the back. For example, when you are wearing the skirt, one side of the split may appear to be longer than the other, or the vent sticks out slightly. This may well be puzzling, especially if you had no difficulty sewing the skirt together.

One tip worth considering is to use interfacing. Cut enough interfacing to cover the area around the vent or split and then fuse it to the wrong side of the fabric on both sides of the back skirt. This stabilizes the area, gives the fabric "body," and results in the vent or split having a crisp finish.

The other alternative is to tack the split closed while you construct the garment; this will help avoid any distortion that arises during the sewing process. Machine stitch the seam to the point at which the split starts, leave about ⅝ inch (1.5 cm) and then tack or machine baste along the fold line of the split to the hem. (The fold line will probably be a continuation of the seam stitching line.)

Leave the tacking stitches in place until you have entirely finished the garment and then unpick them; you will find you will have a straight and even back split.

Question 197:
What's a mitred corner?

A mitred corner can be found on quality garments in areas such as the back vent or slit on skirts and the sleeve hem on jackets, and usually in fabrics like wool crepe and suiting. It's a corner that is cut and pieced together to form an angle and it's an easy way to remove bulk from the corners of seams and hems to give a clean professional finish. The pattern can be altered before you begin your sewing project but only if you are happy with the length; once the mitre is cut you are limiting your options. The mitred corner can also be added during the construction process.

From the wrong side of the garment, turn up the hem and seam allowance. The right sides should be facing each other. Sew across the corner at an angle from point to point. Trim away the excess of the corner and press the seam open.

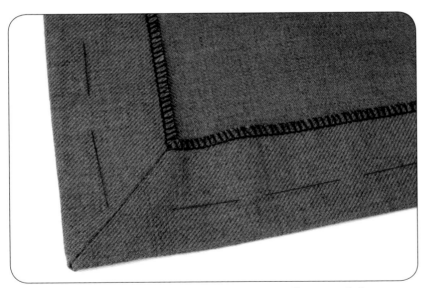

ABOVE A mitred corner reduces bulk on a garment, especially one made from a thicker fabric such as wool suiting.

Question 198:
How do I attach a shoulder pad?

When considering shoulder pads we tend to think of the enormous ones so favored during the 1980s! But used carefully, shoulder pads can define and enhance the shape and silhouette of a garment. Shoulder pads are available in a variety of shapes, thicknesses, and materials.

The commercial sewing pattern will normally make allowances for pad insertion, so make sure the shape and thickness of the shoulder pads you buy correspond to the amount allowed by your pattern. And make sure that when inserted, they don't create wrinkles or folds where none should be.

To find the correct position for the shoulder pad, fold the pad in half at the straight line and mark this with a pin. Then pin the shoulder pad to the shoulder seam of the garment, matching the center of the pad to the center of the sleeve head. Try on the style and adjust the pad to a preferred position if necessary. Stitch the pad to the shoulder seam allowance and to the armhole seam allowance at each side. You don't have to stitch all around the shoulder pad. Just secure to these allowances with a few strong stitches.

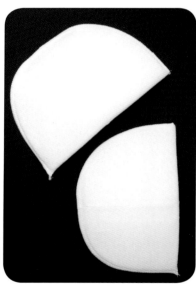

ABOVE Shoulder pads are a cheap notion to buy and add shape and form to a finished garment.

Question 199:
What is "clipping a seam"?

When constructing a garment you will inevitably sew curved seams such as necklines, collars, and cuffs. To ensure that the seam lies flat after sewing and pressing you may have to clip into the seam.

Using small sharp scissors, clip into the seam allowance to ¼ inch (5 mm) from the line of stitching. On an inward curve you may find that the fabric overlaps slightly so you may find it's necessary to snip out small triangles to reduce the bulk.

ABOVE When you clip into a curved seam you will see that the allowance opens out and the garment pieces lie flat after pressing.

Question 200:
How do I sew jersey fabric?

If using jersey, it's important to pick a pattern designed for knit fabrics, as it will account for the stretch of this material and has less ease.

If the jersey is very stretchy, it's worth cutting it out as you would with a slippery fabric (see Question 86). To prevent stretching, use very sharp scissors or a rotary cutter and don't let the fabric "hang" off the cutting table.

Some sewing machines have a special "knit" setting or a deferential feed that helps ensure both the top and bottom layer of your fabric feeds through the machine evenly.

Jersey fabric should be sewn with a ballpoint needle, which slips in between the knitted loops instead of piercing the fabric like a normal "sharp" needle. Seams on jersey fabric should be sewn with a medium-length stretch stitch which many sewing machines have. If not, use a narrow zigzag stitch.

Glossary

Basic blocks
The master pattern drafted to a set of body measurements and is used as a starting point to make other patterns of a similar style.

Bias grain of fabric
The term is used to describe the grainline when it's at a 45-degree angle to the lengthwise and crosswise grain of the fabric.

Crotch length
The measurement taken from your waist at the center front, through the legs, to the waist on the center back.

Curved ruler
See Pattern master.

Cutting layout
The manufacturer's guide to laying pattern pieces on fabric in the most economical way and keeping pieces "on grain" or on fold lines. A number of layout options are provided for different fabric widths and pattern sizes.

Dart
A dart is a wedge-shaped tuck that is taken out of a garment to allow shaping or to remove excess fabric. It's usually found at or under the bust line or on at the waist.

Dress form
A mannequin used to assist in the making up of garments.

Ease or tolerance
The amount of room added to your clothing to make it comfortable for normal activity such as sitting and moving.

Fold line
Used to describe the position of pattern pieces to be placed on the folded fabric. The fabric is folded together, selvedge to selvedge and the pattern piece is placed on the fold line as instructed by the directional arrow marked on the pattern.

Grainline
The fabric grain refers to the direction of the yarns in woven fabric. The straight or lengthwise grain runs along the warp thread, parallel to the selvedges.

Interfacing
A stabilizing fabric used on the wrong side of the fabric to support a piece of the garment, such as a collar or cuff.

Lining
A separate fabric shell made up and inserted into the garment to enclose raw edges and to help the style to keep its shape.

Nap
A fabric with a nap has a "pile" and appears to have different shades; velvet is a fabric with a nap. Layouts are given on the back of the pattern envelope for different fabric quantities for with and without nap.

Notches
Triangular markings on the pattern pieces used to match two corresponding pieces. They can be single, double, or triple.

Notions or Haberdashery
Collective term for a variety of objects and accessories, that includes both items attached to the garment you are making—buttons, zippers and shoulder pads, for example—and sewing equipment—such as thread or seam rippers.

Overlocker or serger
A machine designed to sew and finish edges in one step.

Pattern master or curved ruler
A ruler that provides marked lines for seam allowances and curved angles for armhole readjustments and bust lines. The marked 45-degree line helps when finding the bias grainline.

Pattern terminology
Language used in dressmaking to help the maker with the layout of the fabric and construction of the garment.

Princess seam
The front and back pattern is split into two pieces, the front and the side front pattern as well as the back and side back pattern. The seam or style lines echo the curves of the body.

Seam allowance
The area between the sewing line and the edge of the cloth, normally ⅝ inch (1.5 cm).

Selvedge
The side edges of the fabric. These are often bound more tightly than the fabric weave and are often labeled with the manufacturer's name or fabric content.

Serger
See Overlocker.

Toile
A tester garment made of inexpensive fabric used to check the style and fit of the design.

Useful Contacts and Resources

www.sophie-english.co.uk

www.amybutlerdesign.com
www.burdastyle.com
http://butterick.mccall.com (good for plus sizes)
www.kwiksew.com (good for plus sizes)
www.lauramarshdesigns.co.uk (good for plus sizes)

http://mccallpattern.mccall.com (good for plus sizes)
www.sewgrand.com (specialising in plus sizes)
www.simplicity.com (good for plus sizes)
http://voguepatterns.mccall.com

www.nancysnotions.com
www.sewessential.co.uk

Index

apple (circle) body shape, 36, 37, 38, 39

back adjustments
  bodices and tops, 111-12
  gaping back neck, 119
back-neck to waist
  measurement, 66
  altering patterns, 60, 61
  measuring the pattern, 77
balance of a garment, 195
ball-headed pins, 10
basic tools, 10-11
bias-cut fabrics, 85
  cutting out a skirt, 141
blind hem foot, 20
block patterns, 192-4
bodices and tops, 103-23
  back, 111-12
  bust, 104-10, 122
  buttonhole positions, 123
  discrepancies on patterns, 115
  necklines, 117-21
  shoulders, 113-14, 116
body shape, 36-9
  clothing styles to suit, 38-9
  problem areas, 68, 69
  see also measurements and fit
body size
  adapting a tailor's dummy to, 70
  buying patterns, 43, 58
  determining a good fit, 58, 59
  taking accurate measurements, 58
  see also measurements and fit
bottoms, 134-5
  pants, 171, 187
broad shoulders, 114
bust area
  darts, 104-8, 122, 197
  large busts, 107, 109, 122
  princess seams, 109-10, 197
  small busts, 108, 110
bust measurement, 62, 63
  measuring the pattern, 77
buttonholes, 32, 214
  adjusting positions of, 123
  sewing attachments for, 20
buttons, 32

calico, 72, 194
checked fabrics, 27, 97
chiffon, 100-1
circle body shape, 36, 37, 38, 39
cotton, 24, 87
crotch length, 165-7
cuffs, 161
curved rulers, 16

design ease, 68-9
dress forms, 13
dressmaking shears, 12, 13
dress patterns
  adding sleeves to a sleeveless pattern, 153
  adjusting the waistline position, 128
  joining a bodice and skirt to make, 199

ease and fit, 68-9, 77
embroidery scissors, 12

fabrics, 23-30
  bias, 85
  checked/patterned, 27
  cutting out, 92-3
    jersey/stretch fabrics, 101
    "on the fold," 92
    slippery fabrics, 100-1
    stripes and checks, 96-7
    velvet, 98-9
  "difficult," 23
  and ease, 69
  grain/grainline, 84, 91, 182, 184
  interlining, 30, 46-7
  knit, 25, 26
  linings, 29, 46
  for making toiles, 72
  marking darts and notches on, 94
  marking other features on, 95
  nap, 86, 98-9
  natural or synthetic, 24
  preparing, 17, 87-92
  printed, 23, 83, 92, 98
  right and wrong side, 83
  striped, 23
  tartan, 27, 92
  woven, 25
fabric scissors, 10
facings, 202-3
fasteners, 32
fit see measurements and fit
flared sleeves, 158
fusible interlining, 30

gathered necklines, 121
grain/grainline, 84

and pant patterns, 182, 184
grown-on waistbands, 130-1

hems, 142, 189, 209
  false hems, 201
hips
  adjustments, 137-9
  pants, 172-3
  measurement, 65, 77
hourglass body shape, 36, 37, 38

interfacing, 47
interlinings, 30, 46-7
  fusing, 212
invisible zip-foot, 20
ironing, 87, 99
  pattern pieces, 80-1
irons/ironing boards, 22, 30

jersey/stretch fabrics, 26
  cutting out, 101
  sewing, 219

knit fabrics, 25, 26

linen, 24, 87
lining patterns, 196
linings, 29, 46
  sewing in, 211

marker pens, 17
masking tape, 15
measurements and fit, 57-77
  adapting a tailor's dummy, 70
  altering patterns, 7, 15, 60-1, 75
  determining a good fit, 58, 59
  essential body measurements, 58
  measuring the pattern, 77
  seam allowances, 76, 77
  taking measurements, 62-9
    back-neck to waist, 66, 77
    bust, 62, 63, 77
    hip, 65, 77
    pants, 164, 165-7
    sleeves, 67
    waist, 64
  toiles (tester garments), 71-4
  tolerance or ease, 68-9
measuring tools, 14
mitred corners, 217

nap on fabrics, 86
  cutting out velvet, 98-9
necklines
  adding gathers to, 121
  adjusting patterns, 60
  changing the shape of, 117

checking fit of, 58
gaping, 118-19
loose, 119
stretching, 213
tight, 120
needles, 10-11
sewing machine, 21
notches, 93, 94
notions, 47

over-edge foot, 20, 21
overlocked seams, 19, 207

pants, 163-89
altering for flat bottoms, 187
crease lines on, 186
crotch length, 165-7
fit around the bottom, 171
good fit, 164
hem allowance, 189
hips, 172-3
knee line, 188
large tummies, 167
legs
altering style of pant legs, 181
curving/bending, 174-5
twisting pant legs, 186
lengthening, 177
measuring a crotch seam, 200
pleats, 182-3
reproducing a favourite pair, 200
shortening, 178
side seams swinging back, 184-5
sway backs, 176
thighs, 179-80
waistlines, 168-70
paper
for adapting commercial patterns, 15
patterned fabrics, 27
patterns, 35-55
adapting, 7, 15
block patterns, 192-4
bodices and tops, 103-23
getting lines and angles to meet, 115
joining separate facings, 202
preparations, 82
sequence for, 75
for short people, 61
skirts, 134-43
sleeves and armholes, 145-61
for tall people, 60

pants, 166-89
waistlines, 126-33
back of envelope information, 44-5
and body size, 43, 58, 107
buying, 40-5
calculating amounts of fabric, 46
choosing fabrics, 23
cutting out, 80, 93
checked or plaid material, 97
cutting "on the fold," 92
jersey/stretch fabrics, 101
marking darts and notches, 17, 94
printed fabrics, 98
slippery fabrics, 100-1
striped fabrics, 96
velvet, 98-9
downloading from the internet, 41
information sheet, 48-9
layout plans, 50
level of difficulty, 42
lines and shapes on, 52-5
lining patterns, 196
managing, 196
measuring, 77
numbers printed on pattern pieces, 51
paper scissors for, 11
position of buttonholes on, 123
preparing the fabric, 89-90
preparing the pattern, 80-2
seam allowances, 76
terminology, 49
pear-shaped body type, 36, 37, 38
photocopying patterns, 7
pin cushions, 10
pinking shears, 12
pins, 10, 21
plaid fabrics, 97
pockets, 95, 143
pre-shrinking fabric, 87
pressing, 21-2
princess seams, 109-10, 197
printed fabrics
cutting out, 92, 98
large print, 23
right and wrong side, 83
puff sleeves, 156-7

rectangle body shape, 36, 37, 38
rotary cutters, 12
rulers, 16

satin, 100-1
scissors, 10, 11
seam allowances, 76, 77
cutting out the pattern on fabric, 93, 96
seams, 19, 207
avoiding bulky, 210
clipping, 219
sewing machines, 10, 18
accessories, 20-1
overlockers, 19
threads, 31
shoulder adjustments, 113-14, 116
shoulder pads, 208, 218
silk, 28
cutting out, 101
skirts, 134-43
bias cutting from A-line patterns, 141
false hems, 201
flare on a straight skirt with darts, 198
flat bottoms, 135
grown-on waistbands, 130-1
hemlines, 142
hipline, 137-9
larger bottoms, 134
length, 139-40
pockets in side seams, 143
shortening, 140
slits/vents at back of, 216
sway backs, 136
waistband pieces, 129
sleeve boards (ironing), 22
sleeves and armholes
adding sleeves to a sleeveless pattern, 153
armhole gaping on sleeveless top, 154
broad shoulders, 114
checking fit of, 58
flared sleeves, 158
large upper arms, 148
lengthening a sleeve, 150
making an armhole facing, 152
narrow shoulders, 113
puff sleeves, 156-7
shortening a sleeve, 150-1
short people, 61
sleeve cap, 149
sleeve heads, 208
sleeveless options, 151-2
sleeve measurements, 67
stretching of armholes, 213
taking out gather on a sleeve, 155
tall people, 60
tight armholes, 146-7

Index 223

well-fitting sleeves, 146
wrists, 159-61
slippery fabrics, 100-1
slopers, 193
spot and cross pattern paper, 15
spray starch, 100
steam irons, 22
straightening fabric, 88
straight-stitch foot, 20
striped fabrics, 96
sway backs, 136, 176
synthetic fabrics, 24

tacking, 49, 95
tailor's chalk, 17, 94, 95
tailor's dummies, 13, 70
tailor's ham, 22
tape measures, 14
tartan fabrics, 27, 92
threads, 31

tissue paper patterns
prolonging the life of, 81
toiles (tester garments), 71-4
checking for balance, 195
tolerance and fit, 68-9
top-heavy triangle body type, 36, 37, 38

understitching, 215

Velcro fastenings, 32
velvet, 98-9
V necklines, 117

waistlines, 126-33
adjusting position on dress patterns, 128
"grown-on" waistbands, 130-1
increasing, 126
large tummies, 132
narrow waist with, 122

tightening, 127
pants, 168-70
waistband piece on a skirt pattern, 129
waist measurement, 64
wearing ease, 68
wool, 24
adjusting the neckline, 118
pre-shrinking, 87
woven fabrics, 25
wrists, 159-61

yardsticks, 14

zip foot, 20
zips, 32, 33, 206
marking zip placements, 95

Acknowledgments

cover Quantum Publishing (Caroline Dear); 2 Getty Images/Steve Cole; 9 Shutterstock; 10–12 Quantum Publishing (Marcos Bevilacqua); 13 Shutterstock; 14–16 Quantum Publishing (Marcos Bevilacqua); 18 iStock; 19 Getty Images/Peter Anderson; 20 Getty Images/Dorling Kindersley; 22 Shutterstock; 23 Getty Images/Sarah M. Golonka; 24 Quantum Publishing (Marcos Bevilacqua); 25–26 Shutterstock; 27–28 Quantum Publishing (Marcos Bevilacqua); 29 iStock; 30 Quantum Publishing (Marcos Bevilacqua); 31 Shutterstock; 32 Getty Images/George Doyle; 33 Getty Images/Caro Sheridan/Splityarn; 35 Getty Images/Peter Anderson; 37 Quantum Publishing (euro-design.info); 39 Shutterstock; 41–51 Quantum Publishing (Marcos Bevilacqua); 52– 53 Getty Images/Peter Anderson; 54–55 Quantum Publishing (Marcos Bevilacqua); 57 Shutterstock; 59 Getty Images/Steve Cole; 63–67 Quantum Publishing (euro-design.info); 70–76 Quantum Publishing (Marcos Bevilacqua); 79 Getty Images/Andy Crawford, Steve Gorton; 81–88 Quantum Publishing (Marcos Bevilacqua); 89 Getty Images/Andy Crawford, Steve Gorton; 90–91 Quantum Publishing (Marcos Bevilacqua); 92 Getty Images/Peter Anderson; 93 Quantum Publishing (Marcos Bevilacqua); 94 Getty Images/Peter Anderson; 95–100 Quantum Publishing (Marcos Bevilacqua); 103 (all) Shutterstock; 105–122 Quantum Publishing (Marcos Bevilacqua); 125 (all) Shutterstock; 126–128 Quantum Publishing (Marcos Bevilacqua); 130 Shutterstock; 132–161 Quantum Publishing (Marcos Bevilacqua); 163 Shutterstock; 165 Quantum Publishing (euro-design.info); 166–180 Quantum Publishing (Marcos Bevilacqua); 181 Shutterstock; 182–188 Quantum Publishing (Marcos Bevilacqua); 191–192 Shutterstock; 195–197 Quantum Publishing (Marcos Bevilacqua); 199 Shutterstock; 200–203 Quantum Publishing (Marcos Bevilacqua); 205 Shutterstock; 206–219 Quantum Publishing (Marcos Bevilacqua)